POWER COMMUNICATIONS

POWER COMMUNICATIONS

Positioning Yourself for High Visibility

Valerie Wiener

NEW YORK UNIVERSITY PRESS
New York and London

NEW YORK UNIVERSITY PRESS
New York and London

Library of Congress Cataloging-in-Publication Data
Wiener, Valerie.
Power communications : positioning yourself for high visibility /
Valerie Wiener
p. cm.
Includes bibliographical references and index.
ISBN 0-8147-9273-1
1. Communication in management—Handbooks, manuals, etc.
2. Public relations—Handbooks, manuals, etc.   I. Title.
HD30.3.W54   1994
658.4'5—dc20   93-47480
                                    CIP

New York University Press books are printed on acid-free paper,
and their binding materials are chosen for strength and
durability.

Manufactured in the United States of America

10 9 8 7 6 5 4 3 2 1

To Mom and Dad, for their love, support, encouragement and, especially, inspiration to be a more enriched person each day.

Contents

Acknowledgments

The challenge of writing a book is not one person's alone. Many people influence who we are, what we think, and the work we eventually produce. For me, many very important people helped me accomplish my goal of writing this book and sharing the information inside its covers. It is a pleasure to have this opportunity to thank them.

Certainly, I would not be writing this section if my editor, Niko Pfund, had not demonstrated enough faith in me to publish this text. My profound thanks to him and his able assistant editor, Jennifer Hammer, for all the good-faith work they contributed to the manuscript.

There is no better place than in this text to acknowledge the ongoing influence of my family. My dad, Louis Wiener, Jr., has always reminded me about the value of learning. Every day he affirms that my education is the only part of me that no one can ever take away and, moment by moment, he encourages me to share my knowledge with others. Equally important, he stresses the value of humor to temper life's challenges. My mom, Tui Ava Knight, has been a constant inspiration to me, in life and death. She believed in me enough to smile through the typing of hundreds of essays, short stories, and poems that I crafted from age eight until I could type them myself. She constantly reinforced in me the desire to improve and progress in every personal and professional adventure. My brother, Dr. Paul Knight, has forever motivated me with one of his strongest intellectual talents—to plant seeds of thought in my mind and encourage me to nourish these ideas to fruition.

In addition to my biological family, I have been nurtured by an unbelievable political family and its supporters. U.S. Senator Harry Reid gave me an opportunity, as his press secretary for five years, to learn about government, from the inside out. He helped me effectively share important messages with the people who were affected by them. He also demonstrated to me that to grow we need to be as committed to teaching as to learning. His wife, Landra Reid, enlightened me, through demonstration, about the irreplaceability of the family as a center of support and growth. Maureen Marr, a political consultant I met during Senator Reid's 1986 U.S. Senate campaign, has continued to help me stretch and expand my awareness through her insight and political savvy.

Any credits I want to bestow on people of my past and present would be deficient without including a few special people who inspired me in my craft. Larry Spigelmeyer, my first journalism teacher, taught me that deadlines do not mean the end of the story. He took a fourteen-year-old girl and made her an editor who, on the day of President John F. Kennedy's assassination, put out an eight-page special edition that beat the city newspapers to the street. Roy Vanett, my first city editor, guided me with his high standards, which have continued to serve as a benchmark for my work. He helped me learn that the real substance of the story is the "So what?"—the human factor. Mike Baird, my first cinematographer and television director, openly and skillfully shared his intelligence, expertise, and professionalism. These are just a few of the reasons why he will always serve as a phenomenal role model for me. Victor Carillo, my patient assistant throughout the production of this book, offered input and humor when I needed them most.

My personal and professional evolution as a high-visibility consultant, speaker, and author took root in 1964 when I hosted my first commercial radio talk show. Since then, I have learned the value of people with daily input in my life—people who inspire me to think when I least expect to. These wonderful enthusiasts have been my clients, my students, my teachers, my peers, and my friends. I am particularly proud of the support and idea-sharing that have been offered by Sandra Benbow, Dawn Buffery, Elizabeth Casey, Charlene Herst, David Katzman, Aunt Valerie (Knight), Tom Kubistant, John Kuminecz, Judy Reich, and Idora Silver. All of them have been distinctive contributors to my personal and professional evolution. Their composite influences throughout the years have helped me develop the ideas, principles, and practices that I explain in this book, chapter by chapter.

To you, the readers, I say thank you for your eagerness to master new skills and refine old ones through what you are about to read. Without your support, this book would not have been written.

POWER COMMUNICATIONS

Introduction

Nothing happens unless there is communication. You cannot move unless your brain first communicates with your muscles. You cannot interact with those around you unless you communicate with them and they with you. In fact, without communication, your mind would be an isolated world, unable to take in knowledge or convey it to others.

The ability to communicate extensive and explicit information is one of the characteristics that distinguishes humans from the lower animals. Because our minds are able to communicate with other minds, across space and time, we can keep abreast of the latest social, political, commercial, and technological trends, as well as draw upon history for perspective.

Communication has the power to make things happen. Try to imagine how a factory would run without communication. When the employees arrive, no one tells them what jobs they are to perform, what hours they are to work, and what compensation they are to receive. There are no instructions on the machinery, and there is no one who can tell them how to operate the devices. There are no telephones or fax machines through which inquiries might be made. In fact, there is no mail—either incoming or outgoing.

When, and if, some product is manufactured, nobody on the outside knows about it, because it is not advertised—either in the mass media or by word of mouth. Therefore, there is no demand for the product. If there were a demand, there would be no way of filling it, because the demand has to be communicated through orders. Even if there were orders, they could not be delivered, because to deliver them would require communicating the address of the assignee to the delivery person. Therefore, it should not surprise us to learn that communication skills are at the forefront of requisites for success in business and in almost every other walk of life.

At a time when change is occurring at a dizzying pace, it is all the more important that we stay in touch with the outside world. We need to partake of the shared wisdom of humankind. We cannot merely act as receivers of information. We must perform as transmitters as well. If our minds accumulate all the knowledge and wisdom the human race has compiled over the millenniums, they accomplish nothing unless that wisdom is applied. And that wisdom can be applied only through communication.

When you want to have a positive effect on your community, you must communicate. When you want to rise to the top in your profession or your organization, you must communicate. Communication is power.

The purpose of this book is to help you communicate with power. I show you how to use power communications to become a leader of people.

In chapter 1, I explain what communicating with power involves. This is a natural foundation for chapter 2, in which I describe how to cultivate executive communication skills—the skills that will help you to get ahead in the corporate world. Chapter 3 includes more specific examples of how you can get your message across with high-impact words—words that let you speak with power and precision. I introduce you to public personhood in chapter 4. I discuss several of the integral challenges of public personhood and how you can master them. In addition, public persons are people of accomplishment who are known or recognized by many people whom they themselves do not know. That's why it is particularly important for public persons to put their visibility to work in and for their communities. This takes leadership and, in chapter 5, I discuss how to put this leadership to work in community relations. In chapter 6, I recommend guidelines for communicating through the mass media. Once you are comfortable with these guidelines, you will be ready for chapter 7, in which I explain how you can deal effectively with the media when they come to you for information or for an interview. How to win the interview game is the subject of chapter 8. I will tell you how to deal with difficult, tricky, and hostile questions. I expand my focus on public communication skills in chapter 9 by describing how you can make high-impact executive presentations, before large and small audiences, on formal or impromptu occasions. And, because there are times when you will need to be prepared to communicate about critical situations, I address how to communicate during a crisis in chapter 10. To help you fine-tune your public personhood, chapter 11 details how you can build a well-respected name for yourself. It describes how you can generate and sustain your own public identity.

To many people, communicating itself creates a daunting challenge. This book will help you turn challenges into exciting opportunities. If you think the worlds of media, public speaking, and high visibility pose tough challenges, do not despair. Follow me through this book, and you will learn how to turn these challenges into opportunities.

1

Communicating with Power

To create and sustain a leadership position, you have to communicate with power. To communicate with power, you have to pay conscious attention to the messages you transmit through the way you speak, the way you act, and the way you live. On the basis of these messages, people decide whether you are worthy of being followed. The messages you send are sometimes subtle and sometimes dynamic. Successful leaders learn to use fashion, body language, gestures, and facial expressions to convey powerful unspoken messages. They effectively communicate through one-on-one conversation and public speaking, as well as use the media to extend their messages to large audiences. Successful leaders also identify with the problems and aspirations of the people they want to lead, and communicate images of caring through involvement in their communities.

The instant you encounter another person, you begin communicating. Your dress and physique usually identify you by gender. The color of your skin and eyes, the color and texture of your hair, the shape of your nose and lips, and the structure of your cheekbones send out signals about your racial origins. However, even the strongest physical features can be altered cosmetically to help you change the first impressions you make on others. For example, hair dyes or wigs, contact lenses, cosmetic dentistry, and even plastic surgery can dramatically affect your appearance.

The style and quality of your clothing and accessories give general information about your financial means, your social status, your style-consciousness, and your ability to coordinate colors. The type of clothing you wear tells whether you are likely to be heading for the office or the workbench, a picnic or a funeral, a church service or a cocktail party.

Your posture, your stride, and the way you make eye contact signal whether you are confident or insecure, assertive or passive, modest or arrogant. Your facial expression ordinarily tells whether you are happy or sad, angry or peaceful, excited or bored.

When you speak, you communicate far beyond the literal meaning of your words. Your accent or dialect give clues as to your national or sectional origin. Your volume, pitch, and pace indicate your mood of the moment. A listener will often draw conclusions from subtle signs of face, voice, and posture as to whether you are sincere or devious, concerned or indifferent, truthful or lying. This form of communication is usually done *involuntarily*, without your having to think about it.

The truth is, you cannot *not* communicate. Everything you do and everything you do not do, as well as everything you say and everything you do not say, tell something about you. Effective leaders know this, and they learn how to control the messages they send out, consciously projecting positive images of themselves.

This does not mean practicing deception. No one can get away consistently with projecting a false image. In time, the true image will surface and the false one will be exposed. Good leaders cultivate positive images, carefully live up to them, and take conscious steps to assure that their positive images are widely projected.

You're Always Onstage

High-profile leaders are always onstage, whether they realize it or not. Some experts will tell you that you are under the spotlight from the moment you walk into a room. I have learned from experience that the spotlight reaches beyond the room.

When I give speeches, I put myself in my "speech mode" several blocks from the location, while I am still driving my car. When I get out, I practice "positive poise" with every person I encounter—valet parkers, bellhops, restaurant personnel, and so forth—before I ever walk through the door of the meeting room. By the time I reach the room, I am primed for the presentation.

It is my practice to arrive early enough to find

where I am supposed to be, survey the room, set up my visual aids, and be available as the first person enters the room. Once, prior to a seminar at a local college, I found myself completely turned around and could not locate the room. I finally spotted two women in a lounge area and, in a make-light-of-the-moment way, asked for assistance. They directed me to the other end of the building. After I arrived and got settled, the first women to enter my room were the two who had rescued me from limbo. If I had shown anger or frustration to those women when we had first met, you can bet they would not have believed one word of my presentation. It was entitled, "How to Deal with Negative People and Frustrating Events."

It's the Perception That Counts

Not all the signals we send out involuntarily are necessarily accurate. The person who appears to be of Asian descent may in fact be a Native American. You may think you are looking at an African-American when, in fact, you are looking at a Nigerian or a Haitian. The person who appears to be glum may be happy on the inside. Some people of moderate means manage to dress in a way that says "money." Some uncommonly wealthy people are uncommonly slovenly in their dress and personal habits. A native of Georgia can cultivate the speech patterns of a midwesterner.

Whether the signals you transmit are accurate or misleading, people will respond to you on the basis of their *perceptions*. If they perceive you to be angry, they will respond to you in the way they normally respond to angry people. If you send them what they think is a threatening message, people will react to the perceived threat. When your listeners assume you are successful, they will behave around you the way they do around successful people. If, on the other hand, you give them the impression that you are a failure, you can expect your listeners to treat you that way.

An experiment outside an office building in a large city serves to illustrate this point. A man dressed as a prosperous businessman accosted passersby and told them he had left his wallet at home and needed money to catch the commuter train. The passing businesspersons responded generously. Some not only gave him train fare, but also insisted on adding enough for a drink in the club car. Before the day was out, the man had collected $600.

On another day, he appeared at the same building dressed casually, telling the same story. His collections were far less than on the previous occasion. Some people rebuked him for being so careless.

Finally, the individual appeared in shabby, down-and-out attire and gave the same story. He received no sympathy and no money.

In each case, the passersby were dealing with the same individual with the same personality and the same financial means. But they had different *perceptions* on each occasion, and those perceptions dominated their responses in determining whether they gave him money.

This same principle applies in other pursuits besides panhandling. In whatever endeavor you engage yourself, people will respond to you on the basis of their perceptions. These perceptions are based on the way you communicate.

To exert affirmative leadership, you must learn to communicate positive, powerful images. Furthermore, to *be* a leader, people have to *perceive* you as a leader. "Successful leadership depends far more upon the follower's perception of the leader's abilities than upon the leader's own perceptions," observed James M. Kouzes and Barry Z. Posner, writing in the magazine *Management Review.*[1]

Two recent presidencies make the point. Few objective critics would rate Jimmy Carter as intellectually inferior to Ronald Reagan. Many would rate Carter as among the brighter of our presidents, while most would put Reagan in the middle ranks, at best. Yet few would challenge the proposition that Reagan was the more powerful president, even though Carter's party controlled Congress throughout his presidency while Reagan's party had to settle for control of only one house for most of his term. The difference can be found in perceptions. Reagan lived up to his title as "the Great Communicator," and Americans perceived him as a decisive leader. They perceived in Carter an earnest uncertainty.

Powerful leaders must project powerful images. They need to decide what types of images they want to project, then use the power of communication intelligently to project those images.

What Managers Look for in Leaders

When Kouzes and Posner polled more than 7,500 managers nationwide on the qualities they admire in their leaders, several characteristics they perceive to be important relating to communications cropped up frequently.[2] Among them were:

- Honesty.

- Ability to inspire.

- Ability to understand the perspectives of others.

- Willingness to stand up for what they believe.

- Ability to speak with passion.

The Handshake That Lost an Election

Alex Seith, who came close to defeating U.S. Senator Charles Percy of Illinois in 1978, learned the importance of perceptions, to his deep chagrin.

Seith was to appear with Percy on a Chicago television talk show. He was fuming over a Percy campaign ad that implied that Seith had unsavory connections with the Mafia. Often, when guests on this talk show made newsworthy comments, the television station would use excerpts in its newscasts. Therefore, it customarily filmed the talk-show guests as they entered the building and continued the filming right up to the time of the show. This footage would serve as lead-ins for the newscast.

Seith arrived at the set before Percy did, and while the news cameras were running, he expressed his anger at the Percy ad. "I'm not making any physical contact with him, not even shaking hands," he said.

"I'll say what I want to say and not make physical contact."

A Seith aide later walked up to the candidate and whispered something into his ear. The talk-show host said the aide told Seith to shake hands with Percy if he walked onto the set. When the senator appeared, Seith shook his hand. Then, with cameras still running, though the show had not started, Seith called his wife to the set and asked Percy to explain to her why he had run the ad. Mrs. Seith cried. Percy asked Seith to hold his remarks and discuss the issue "publicly," meaning during the show.

After the show, Percy went into the hallway and, before reporters and cameras, apologized for the ad. He said he had not seen it before publication, and he promised to remove it from all other editions and newspapers scheduled to carry the ad. Then he fainted.

This gave the television station the news peg it needed to run all the pre-show and post-show footage.[3] Viewers heard Seith say he would not shake hands with Percy or have any other physical contact with him. Then they saw him warmly shake hands with the senator. They saw Seith angrily confronting the senator, then saw Percy calmly deal with the anger.

Seith undoubtedly meant it when he said he would not shake hands with Percy. But he later accepted his aide's advice and went through with the handshake. Viewers may have perceived this as saying one thing and doing another. Seith went into the talk show with a solid lead in the polls. On election day, he lost.

Leaders Inspire through Public Speaking

Followers look for leaders who are inspiring as well as honest. It takes more than a dream to motivate people; leaders must be able to communicate vision, action, and desired results to inspire people to follow them.

That's why Patricia Aburdene, coauthor of *Megatrends 2000*, lists public speaking among the prime qualifications for the CEO of the twenty-first century.

Aburdene recommends that organizations create corporate visions to provide a clear picture of where they want to go. "A corporate vision, however, remains just that until the CEO can bring it to life by communicating it to the only people who can carry it out: the firm's human resources," she writes. "But they have got to be sold on the idea first."

"Persuasive writing can accomplish part of the job. But to really inspire people, there is nothing like a damn good speech."[4]

Accomplished leaders learn to "connect" their images with the perceptions of those they want to lead. That means learning to see things from the other's perspective—actually to know how the other person sees and feels things.

I have spent enough time working with politicians in Washington to know that you cannot make this connection if you stay on your side of the fence, always looking at your own garden. You have to jump over that fence, into your neighbors' backyards. You have to walk barefoot through their soil and grass, and experience the world through the eyes and the soles of your neighbors. You have to learn to speak their language and identify with their dreams.

Before you can build a relationship with the people you hope to lead, you will need to know who these people are, as well as their beliefs, likes and dislikes, expectations, fears and prejudices, hopes and dreams, and more. Only when you know them this well, and continue to grow in your knowledge of them and their interests, can you expect them to follow you.

Michael McCall and Michael Lombardo of the Center for Creative Leadership in Greensboro, North Carolina, conducted a study of executives who were derailed during their careers. They found that ability—or inability—to understand other people's perspectives was the most glaring difference between those who arrived and those who were derailed.

Be a Leader in Your Community

To be a leader in business or in politics, you must first contribute leadership to your community. Community organizations and community causes are the breeding grounds for national leaders. They form power bases from which you can project your image onto ever larger screens. Teddy Roosevelt was president of the New York City Board of Police Commissioners before he became governor, vice president, and president. Harry S Truman worked as a postmaster and a road overseer in Missouri before he became a senator, vice president, and president. Remember, you will need to make good in your own backyard before you can make good in bigger pastures. In politics, it has become axiomatic that if you cannot carry your home precinct, you are unlikely to win the election.

By the same token, if you cannot command the respect of the people in your community, you are unlikely to command the respect of the people in your corporation. It should not surprise you that when corporations look for executive material, they look for community involvement as well as corporate accomplishment. The two generally go hand in hand.

Leadership in any organization goes to those who stand for something and are willing to speak passionately about it. In many cultures, people appreciate and respond to leaders who formulate a position and stand by it. We tend to follow people who demonstrate confidence in their own decisions and actions. When leaders are vague about beliefs and values they create stress for those who look to them for direction. Followers need to know what to expect. Otherwise, confusion, apathy, conflict, indecision, and antagonism can result.

True leaders stand by what they believe in, regardless of whether their beliefs accord with the popular view. If these views are honest, with solid and reasonable arguments behind them and an ethical foundation beneath them, you will find people who will be willing to follow you.

Knowing what you believe is not enough. You must be willing to speak with passion about the things you believe in. Equally important, in gaining the commitment of others, the leader must be able to communicate enthusiasm, energy, and dedication.

So the route to establishing and nurturing a positive identity and enhancing a creative image in your profession and community starts at *community relations*.

I define community relations as the kinship between you and your community—the extent to which you have walked barefoot through your neighbors' yards.

Cultivating this kinship will result in rewards for you, your business or profession, and your community. It will strengthen your ability to increase your business, to advance in your career, and to achieve wider recognition as an individual. It will also help make your community a better and more prosperous place in which to live and work.

Expanding Identity

I have seen this demonstrated often through the experiences of clients. One of them had a radio show that broadcast valuable information about real estate transactions. His two-and-a-half-minute show ran daily in prime time on an all-news radio station. At first, he asked me to help him refine his scripts. But my role expanded as we developed more opportunities for him to enjoy positive visibility.

First, we restructured the program to include a stronger focus on the host as an expert—a specialist whose know-how was unique to his community. We wrote the program from the perspective of an *expert* giving advice that benefits the listener. The advice was based on what the audience needed and not on what the expert wanted the audience to know. This established the real-estate expert as a person who listens and responds to the information others share with him. This approach had a positive impact on the people who heard the program and on my client's business.

We also expanded my client's identity in the community in new environments. He became a speaker for the school district. He began participating in a program with other community leaders to encourage at-risk students to stay in school. Now other high-profile people perceive him as someone who gives something back to the community. They also see him as someone they know and trust.

To establish a more broad-based identity in your community, whether the community is a geographical neighborhood or a corporate setting, look for unique avenues for positive visibility.

Another one of my clients, the owner/operator of a large rent-a-car business, wanted to establish herself in the community. She wanted her identity to extend beyond her own industry. So we worked out a plan that would project her humanitarian side, thus giving her a balanced identity of "a strong businessperson who cares."

I designed her program on three levels:

- **Community service.** This became a natural foundation for her new visibility. We developed a workshop series for women reentering the work force. On Christmas and Easter, she donated her time, her home, and her culinary talents to troubled children from the county's foster-care facility. She was also elected to the board of the Women's Council of the Chamber of Commerce.

- **Media.** I trained her in media skills and awareness to help her deal positively with her expanded identity. I developed a one-year media plan that included news releases, media appearances, public service announcements, and more. She was able to establish a positive identity as an expert in her field and a leader of community projects.

- **Identity maintenance.** Regularly, we fine-tuned her identity skills with training and review in interview techniques, presentation skills, participation in one-time-only events, and refinement of her interactive people skills.

Using the Media

As we have seen, establishing a high-visibility image requires effective use of two avenues of mass communication: the public speech and the media.

Public speaking provides the opportunity to communicate with people in large and small groups and to rub elbows with them before and afterwards. The media give you access to much larger audiences. The key is to know how to gain access to them.

Several years ago I had a client who wanted me to develop a media campaign for his young business—his first mailbox outlet. As we talked, I discovered that he had made a strong commitment to environmental protection. He told me that he air-popped popcorn for use as a packaging material. He did not use styrofoam, because it was not biodegradable. He felt that he could make a stronger contribution to environmental protection with popcorn. We checked and discovered that he was the only business owner among this company's 1,500 outlets nationwide who used popcorn as a packaging filler.

We had an angle for a feature story. My client had an opportunity to set himself and his business apart. We sent out a news release describing his unusual contribution to ecology. Newspapers and television stations across the country picked up the story. My client had set himself apart from the ordinary run of entrepreneurs, establishing himself as a businessperson with a conscience. The publicity also bestowed upon him the image as a successful business leader in the community. And the community, of course, benefited from his unusual commitment to the environment.

If you take the time to learn what the media look for in news and feature articles and programs, you will find many occasions to take advantage of the large audiences the media command.

Communication: The Essence of Leadership

To lead, you must point a direction and speak and act so that people want to follow you. Thus, communication is the essence of leadership. In succeeding chapters we will deal extensively with ways of cultivating positive avenues of communication.

In Summary:

• You cannot *NOT* communicate. You are constantly sending out nonverbal signals that trigger perceptions in others.

- Effective leaders develop an awareness of the signals they are sending out and use them to project powerful, positive images.

- The qualities people look for in leaders involve communication. They include honesty, ability to inspire, ability to identify with others, a willingness to stand for something, and an ability to speak up with passion.

- The place to begin building your powerful positive image is in your own neighborhood through community involvement.

- Two powerful means of image building are public speaking and media mastery.

Notes

1. James M. Kouzes and Barry Z. Posner, "The Credibility Factor: What Followers Expect from Their Leaders, *Management Review*, January 1990, 29.
2. Ibid., 30.
3. Jack Hilton and Mary Knoblauch, *On Television: A Survival Guide for Media Interviews* (New York: Amacom, 1980), 50–55.
4. Patricia Aburdene, "How to Think Like a CEO for the '90s," *Working Woman*, September 1990, 136.

2

Cultivating Executive Communication Skills

ow that we have learned the necessity for cultivating a power image, let's begin to explore ways of bringing that image to life. To do so, you have to learn to make everything people see in you, hear from you, and sense in you convey the message you want to convey. Effective leaders turn purposeful communication into power.

In fact, estimates indicate that 85 percent of your success in business depends on effective communication and interpersonal skills. And 80 percent of the lost business in America is lost because employees express attitudes of indifference to prospective clients or customers.

When a customer comes in with a complaint and the customer service representative communicates an attitude of indifference, hostility, or helplessness, the business is likely to lose a customer. And when a customer walks away angry, you have not just lost a sale. You may have lost *every* sale you might ever have made to that customer. Over a lifetime, that can add up to a lot of dollars. That does not even take into consideration the sales you will never make to people influenced by your disgruntled customer.

Today's customers are putting less emphasis on what your *product* can do for them and more emphasis on what your *company* can do for them. Therefore, the company that communicates a confident, competent, and caring attitude is more likely to get the customer, even if its products are no better than, or even marginally inferior to, those of a competitor with poorer communication skills.

It is up to the executive to set the tone for proper communications and to act as a role model in power communications.

A Complex Process

As we saw in chapter 1, communication does not start when you open your mouth. It starts when you come into the presence of another. Communication is a complex process that conveys information and defines relationships. When you communicate, you are trying, consciously or unconsciously, to change the other person. Smart leaders learn to use communication consciously to bring about changes that are favorable to their interests.

The great majority of the communication you do is nonverbal. According to a study conducted by Albert

T. Mehrabian, about 55 percent of your communication consists of body language. You also communicate by the quality of your voice, which comprises 38 percent of your communication. Only about 7 percent of the information you convey consists of words and their meanings.

So let's assume that you have decided to take charge of your personal communication. You want to *choose* the messages you send to others. You do not want to leave 93 percent of your communication to unconscious habits and reflexes. Where do you start?

Start with the Eyes

Let's start with the eyes. Many experts will tell you that eye contact is the most important means of nonverbal communication.

Think of the people with whom you have difficulty communicating. How many of them habitually look you directly in the eye? Avoiding eye contact is a sign of low self-esteem. When you were a child and were being less than honest with your parents, did you look them in the eye? It is hard to maintain self-esteem while being dishonest, and few people can lie while looking directly into the eyes of the person they are lying to. When you were scolded as a child, where did you look? Probably at the floor. You could not bear to look into the condemning eyes of your mother or father or teacher. People maintain a higher degree of eye contact with those they believe will approve or support them.

Poor eye contact also communicates weakness. It is

easier for people so inclined to run roughshod over those who will not look them in the eye.

Yevgeny Yevtushenko, the Russian poet, once visited an American home where a magnificent moose head was on display.

"How could you bear to kill such a marvelous creature?" asked the poet.

"He didn't look me in the eye," explained his host.

When you shake hands with other people or say greetings to them, look them fully in the eye. The message you convey will vary, depending upon your other body language. At minimum it says, "I am respectfully acknowledging your presence, I am accepting you as a peer, I intend to be honest and open with you, and you have my attention for the duration of our encounter."

During conversation, maintain open and honest eye contact, but do not overdo it. Long, steady contact can make people uncomfortable. A relaxed and steady gaze at the other person, looking away occasionally, helps make the conversation more personal and enhances the directness of your message.

Next Comes Posture and Distance

Now that you have trained your eyes to convey your self-confident message, let's look at your posture. The way you stand, sit, and walk conveys a two-sided message: it tells people what you think of yourself, and lets them know what you think of them.

Your posture will vary between two extremes:

slouching and rigidity. The person who slouches is conveying a message of indifference. If you do not stand erect in the presence of another person, you are saying, "You do not matter enough for me to assume an alert posture in your presence. Nothing you say or do is likely to interest me, and I'm not going to let you interfere with my relaxation."

The person who stands rigid and tense is conveying a message of anxiety and insecurity. If you stand like a soldier on guard duty, you are saying, "I do not feel comfortable in your presence. I do not quite trust you; therefore, I am going to keep my guard up just in case you try to put something over on me."

An active, erect posture while facing the other person gives assurance that you are alert to what the other has to communicate and that you are prepared to respond. Such a posture lends additional assertiveness to your message.

Note that I am not saying "never slouch" or "never stand rigid," or "always stand alert and erect." You should be aware that each of these postures conveys its own message. If the message you want to convey is one of indifference or disdain, go ahead and slouch. If you want the other person to believe that you are anxious and insecure, assume your guard-duty pose. Just be alert to the posture you have assumed and of the messages you are sending.

Your distance from the person with whom you are communicating also sends a message. Standing or sitting unusually close to another person implies intimacy. When this intimacy is unwarranted, it can cause discomfort. Some people use this technique to dominate others through territorial moves.

Communicating with the Hands

Now that you are sending the messages you want to send with your eyes and your posture, let's try for some communication with the hands. Gestures can add emphasis, openness, and warmth to your message. When you converse with an animated conversationalist, note the hands. They move in easy, natural, but lively gestures that reinforce and enhance the spoken words. Relaxed use of hand gestures adds depth and power to your message. Uninhibited movement also suggests openness, self-confidence, and spontaneity on your part. Good speakers use two kinds of gestures: *descriptive* and *emphatic.*

Descriptive gestures literally illustrate your point in the air. How thick was the research file? Your hands automatically spread apart vertically to show the approximate depth, even as you describe it verbally: "It was two feet deep if it was an inch." How big were the hailstones? Your thumb and index finger form an oval as you describe them: "They were about the size of pigeon eggs."

Emphatic gestures serve to emphasize or underscore specific points in your speech. Your hand moves up and down in hammer-like fashion to drive home your point. Or your arm moves outward, palm open, as you deliver an explanation.

The timing of gestures is important. I once worked with an elected official at the national level who demonstrated how easy it is for nonverbal communications to contradict the spoken message, and therefore to convey a misleading impression.

He was addressing a group of agitated voters on a very sensitive issue that would have a significant impact on their lives. As he talked about "those people who want to inflict this disastrous decision on you," he pointed to himself. He was still pointing to himself as he spoke of "those of us who oppose this matter," but the subtle message had already been flashed to his listeners. By pointing to himself too early, he identified himself in their minds with "those people" who were trying to inflict an injustice on the voters.

Another example of awkward hand gestures involved Governor Michael Dukakis during his presidential campaign in 1988. He had a tendency to clench his fingers into a semi-fist, palms up, with thumbs pointed upward. He steadily moved his fists up and down, back and forth, which created mixed impressions. His audience often got annoyed with the redundant gesture and also saw Dukakis as insecure about his message.

And the Face

The face eloquently conveys information and powerfully shapes image. Early in my media career, I watched the coverage of the assassinations of John F. Kennedy and his brother Robert. As I observed the faces of the television newscasters, I noticed something very subtle but very powerful in their demeanors. Their messages were devastating and numbing; many of the newscasters I watched demonstrated their compassion, often through their tears. However, they also handled their messages with authority through their facial expressions. They showed their humanity *and* their strength by demonstrating the same kind of control a parent would show a child during a family trauma. This facial body language, at a time of particular national vulnerability, gave the viewers a lifeline of hope and direction.

Their faces conveyed their inner feelings. Most of the time, the inner feeling you want to project is warmth and cheerfulness. Therefore, I counsel all of my high-visibility clients to smile when appropriate. If you say something with a smile, 90 percent of the time your listeners will smile with you. Even in a serious dialogue, turn on the softer side of yourself. A poker face is boring—unless you are involved in an intense poker game. Show a glimmer of hope in the eyes. Display an "open face." Why? Because when "experts" speak, we look to them for the answers. When we see people on television responding to situations or issues, these interviewees are the experts on the subject. However difficult the information is to handle, we, the audience, look to these spokespersons for answers and, especially, hope. If these people let their own emotions overpower them, then all they convey is negativity, uncertainty, or both. And no matter what the vocal message, the facial expression tells a doomsday story.

The Impact of Your Voice

Next, let's consider your voice. When you speak, you are communicating a rich texture of meaning that goes far beyond the literal definitions of words. Your voice quality—tone, inflection, volume, pace, pitch, breathing, and even pausing—conveys 38 percent of your meaning.

Not all men can speak in the rich, rumbling voice of Charles Kuralt or in the organ tones of the late Senator Everett Dirksen. Not all women speak with the ease and authority of Connie Chung or poet laureate Maya Angelou. But all of us can pitch our voices in such a way as to deliver the most effective tones. The key is to know what tone is comfortable and effective for you. You can accomplish this by working with a speech coach to help you determine your natural range.

When you are being assertive, use the lower end of your voice range. The low pitch sends the message that you are in control of your emotions and of the situation. A high-pitched voice conveys excitement, perhaps tinged with nervousness, fear, or insecurity. A shrill voice denotes lack of control.

Avoid speaking in a monotone. Vary your pitch and pace to show a range of emotions, but do not let your voice climb too high. This can result in a loss of credibility.

Adjust the volume of your voice to fit the message you are conveying. Your voice can thunder with outrage or whisper with drama. It can rise in measured increments as you build toward a climax.

Fluency is another element in voice quality. A hesitant, stammering delivery conveys uncertainty and a lack of mastery of your subject. President George Bush demonstrated the impact of this principle during his 1992 campaign for reelection. The *New Republic* included a weekly column devoted to "Bushisms"— inarticulate utterings and stammerings that epitomized Bush's leap-from-one-thought-to-another style.

In comparison, his opponent, Arkansas Governor Bill Clinton, presented his messages eloquently, thoughtfully, and clear-mindedly; he completed thoughts and delivered entire sentences.

Clear, slow comments are more easily understood and are usually more powerful than rapid-fire deliveries, or speech that comes in erratic bursts. Keep your comments moving. Long hesitations encourage your listeners to disengage from your conversation and let their minds wander elsewhere.

Onstage, they say, timing is everything; it isn't quite. We have already enumerated several other aspects of communication that also are important to those who wish to exercise power through their messages. Much of the effectiveness of what you say, however, does rely on the timing. If you hesitate to speak up, the moment of opportunity may pass. If you speak too soon, you may catch your audience unprepared and unwilling to listen.

Your Clothes and Body Type Send a Message

Finally, what you wear and how you wear it sends powerful signals to those around you. Your clothing and accessories reflect your status: who you think you are and what you want others to think about you.

Kayte Van De Mark of Visual Design Management in Reno, Nevada, provides some expert advice on choosing styles and colors for maximum positive impact. In most business settings, the idea is to blend in rather than to stand out. If you are a man working in Dallas, your string tie and western boots might blend with the crowd in your office tower. In Boston, such a costume would mark you as different, and maybe a little eccentric. If eccentricity is the image you want to convey, wear the boots and string tie in Beantown, and even don a Stetson if you wish. Be aware, however, of what you are saying with this apparel.

The same applies to women's attire. The bright California style in women's clothes might go well in Santa Barbara, but in Manhattan a more subdued look might be in order.

Many people have a natural eye for colors. If you do not, you can find professional guidance in top-quality clothing stores. Or you can seek the advice of a friend or spouse who does have an eye for color.

You can also educate yourself by reading fashion magazines and noting what is in style, and by observing the attire of successful people in your organization. Remember to select your wardrobe based on what suits you best, not what looks good on a professional model.

While fashions may vary from season to season, there are some constants. Your clothing is most attractive when it repeats your natural shape. When you try to wear something that opposes your natural shape, you send mixed signals.

There are five basic body shapes: round, long-oval, angular, oval, and soft-angle. Trace the appropriate shapes and determine one that is dominant in you. Or have a friend help you decide your body shape. This tells you your body "design." When you repeat this design in hair style, eyewear, clothing, accessories, home and office decor, presentation techniques, and props, you have reached your visual power potential.

Know Your Colors and Patterns

Color, as well as shape, plays a prominent role in style. The colors that you wear should look like you. They should reflect your uniqueness and accentuate your natural attractiveness. A "color" is a hue that moves, animates, and clarifies your natural coloring. It should create a mood and make a statement. You can influence your appearance by regulating the colors that you wear and how you wear them. If you are speaking to a small group in a small room with an intimate setting, your color message must match this occasion by not upstaging and overpowering the audience and environment. You definitely want to be remembered for who you are, and not for the clothes you are wearing. You create a lasting impression when you achieve visual harmony.

A "palette" is a collection of color that expresses all of your needs and meets all of your requirements. All your colors go together on you. You are the coordinating factor. Your colors will always be your colors, even when your skin tans or your hair turns to silver. Selecting your palette goes beyond the scope of personal preference or common sense. Color analysis spans art details and color principles. It ultimately affects what people see. When people look at you, their eyes mix your coloring with the colors you are wearing. If the result is pleasing, you will sustain their attention.

One of the secrets of effective visual communication lies in the way you use mood. Mood heightens or plays down your individuality, depending upon the occasion. Let the occasion determine the mood. You can also handle mood through color. When you become more enlightened about the impact of visual communication, you can learn to set the mood you want to project, and thereby control it.

Clothing patterns can be evaluated by their degree of serious or carefree attitude. Solids are the most serious, creating stability and character. They set forth no movement or emotional association. Plaids and prints are the most whimsical and spirited. They are intense in their motion to the eye and indicate a lack of focus. You can use them very effectively when you properly evaluate the subject, the occasion, the mood, and the environment in which you will wear them. Remember to choose the right pattern for the right occasion, or you will create an incongruity in your communications. When you use patterns effectively, you will definitely enhance your individuality and impact.

How you dress is strictly a personal decision, but it is not a private one. Your choice of clothing advertises itself—and you. The best policy allows you to dress to feel comfortable with yourself. Avoid extremes, unless you are in the business of attracting attention to your appearance.

Aggressive, Submissive, or Assertive?

As an executive or aspiring executive, your words, voice, and body language will project one of three images of you. They will portray you either as aggressive, submissive, or assertive.

Aggressive people express themselves in ways that intimidate, demean, or degrade other people. Aggressive people bully and manipulate. Aggressive behavior puts people on guard. People responding to aggressive acts are more likely to respond defensively than cooperatively. If you are an aggressive executive, your employees are more likely to create cover stories for their actions when things go wrong than to look for workable solutions.

Submissive or passive people are reluctant or unable to express their thoughts and feelings with confidence. Such behavior builds disdain or contempt in others. If you convey a message of submissiveness, people will look for ways to use you instead of for ways to help you.

Passive people are forever pretending. Just to please others, they will pretend to prefer one thing, when they really prefer another. If you say to a passive follower, "Let's start the project tonight," that passive person might say, "Sounds good to me," when the real sentiment is "Can't we wait till tomorrow? I'm tired."

Passive workers fill in for their colleagues time after time, often to the detriment of their own tasks, and pretend they are happy to do it. They pay dearly for being so "nice."

Learning assertiveness can liberate you. When you

become assertive, you drop this pretense. You do not stop doing favors, but you let it be known that you will not be "used," and you make it clear where the line is to be drawn. Assertive people have confidence in themselves, look out for themselves, and like themselves. They get more out of life because they insist on living the lives that they want to live. The art of assertiveness is staking out your own position without preempting the positions of others.

Each human is entitled to individual "space." As poet W. H. Auden expressed it:

> *Some 30 inches from my nose,*
> *The frontier of my person goes.*

Assertive people do not trespass on the private space of others. They do not pry into private matters that do not concern them and do not try to impose their private standards on others. When you do that, you have gone beyond assertiveness and into the realm of aggressiveness.

Assertive people guard their own space against intruders. They do not allow others to infringe upon them, their values, or their own preferences within that personal space. They do not allow put-downs by others to rob them of their confidence in those values or to undermine their self-esteem.

Once you enter into a relationship with another person, you create another circle of space that encompasses the relationship. Each individual still has private space, but a new, larger space now exists in which the two interact. For that interaction to be healthy, both persons have to state clearly where they stand and what they want from the relationship. This is an essential part of public personhood.

If you are constantly deferring to the other partner without asserting your own wants and needs, you are being passive. You cannot exert leadership while being passive. In a healthy relationship, both partners assert their wants and needs and the two develop a system of give-and-take in which neither dominates the other or intrudes upon the other's private space.

Assertive individuals seek out relationships beyond their own private space. They become active in community organizations and activities and seek to have impact on the larger world. They do this by determining where they stand and letting this be known in positive, constructive ways.

To be assertive means to communicate with confidence and honesty whatever you think, feel, and believe. It means standing up for your own rights while respecting the rights of others.

Assertiveness is a positive and constructive form of communication that will enhance your personal and professional life. It offers an alternative to the opposing extremes of submissiveness and aggression. Assertiveness deals with power on a personal level in every environment and is rooted in self-respect and in respect for others.

Resolving Conflicts

Most people know that assertive behavior can lead them into conflict when they interact with others. Public persons, however, recognize the value of assertive behavior and put it to use to benefit the most people.

When tackling conflict, assertive people work toward equitable resolutions. For example, when you defend your own space against an intruder, the intruder's response is likely to be defensive. No one likes to be told, "You're standing on my turf and I want you off."

The best way to deal with such situations is to prepare for them in advance. You begin by describing the behavior you would like to see changed. You tell how the behavior makes you feel and how it affects you. Then you describe a behavior that is more satisfactory to you.

These statements need to be "I" centered. You do not pass judgment on the other person. You simply describe how that person's behavior affects you in an unsatisfactory way. To make sure that you are removing all the judgmental words from your message, write it down ahead of time. Analyze it and fine-tune it until you know exactly what you want to say. Then become thoroughly familiar with the message so that you can deliver it in its most effective form. Do not expect the person you are dealing with to become suddenly contrite and apologetic. Human nature might prevent an immediate change.

Assertive communication is tailored to the person and the situation with which you are dealing. It consists of sending "I" messages rather than "you" messages. "You" messages are often offensive, insensitive, nonproductive, and barrier-producing: *"You* ought to do that differently." "If *you* would only show a little more interest in what you are doing." *"You* ought to throw that idea out and look for something creative."

"I" messages consist of statements that describe you—expressions of your feelings and experiences.

These expressions must be authentic, honest, and congruent, for they express your inner reality. Remember, though, that the inner reality they express is yours, not that of the other person. So your "I" messages will not contain judgments, evaluations, or interpretations of others.

Successful "I" messages require that you know what you want and need in life and in the specific situations you face. Through them, you take personal responsibility for meeting your preferences. When you communicate with "I" messages, you are not putting the blame on others; you are putting the responsibility on yourself. "I" messages express your preferences in ways that make others want to cooperate with you to meet your needs. When you use "I" messages, be willing to listen if the other person becomes defensive.

Effective assertive communication is characterized by a basic four-part message. It consists of:

1. A *nonjudgmental description* of the behavior to be changed.

2. A *disclosure* of the asserter's feelings.

3. A *clarification* of the concrete and tangible effect of the other person's behavior on the asserter.

4. A *description* of a behavior that is more satisfactory to you. An assertive statement, then, might progress from *"When you . . ."* to *"I feel. . ."* to *"because . . ."* to *"I prefer . . ."*

Let's say that an employee is chronically late for work and you decide it is time for a talk. A "you" message might go like this:

> *You are always late, and when you get here you waste time talking to your colleagues. You interrupt the entire office. You are lazy and unproductive, and you are going to have to change.*

With that kind of approach, you are going to have an angry and defensive employee. Now apply the formula for "I" messages:

> **When you constantly arrive late, I feel** that you are affecting the productivity of the rest of us, **because** others get behind when you disrupt their work. **I prefer to see** you arrive early enough to make sure you are effectively organized to begin your day at 8:30 A.M.

This four-part message can help you to build a rapport with your team while getting your message across. Sometimes, however, you will need to be more forceful and less personal with your message. In these situations you might consider using the four-part message but exclude the words "I feel" from the assertive statement.

Changing Others' Behavior

As an assertive leader, you will need to provide guidance, direction, and correction to others. This means bringing about changes in others' behavior. Four guidelines will help you accomplish these goals:

1. *Speak up.* You have to state your need or desire. Tell people what you want them to do. This guideline is often difficult to carry out because we often assume that the other person "ought to know." Sometimes it is necessary to repeat a request, and many people are reluctant to do this. Often, however, the person to whom you made the request will forget it or relegate it to a low priority. If you do not repeat it, you increase the probability that nothing will change.

2. *Put the request in the form of an "I" message.* When you start your message with *"You* should" or *"You* must" or *"You* don't need to," the person receiving the message will perceive you as finger-pointing and shoving. This will produce resistance and defensiveness. Never open with "Why didn't *you.* . . . ?" You will get a long list of reasons, excuses, and alibis, none of it being what you really want.

A message that begins with *"I* need," or *"I* must have," or *"I* would find it most helpful if," or "What *I* am expecting in this situation is" will be far more likely to get results. Messages stated this way sound more like invitations than commands.

3. *Aim your messages at the present or the future, and not at the past.* No one can deliver yesterday. The only time over which the receiver of your message has any control is the present or the future. If you want something done, it will have to be done in one of those time frames. If you aim your request toward the here and now or the soon-to-be here and now, your request is far more likely to be honored.

4. *Be specific.* Do not deal in generalities. This is the most difficult guideline to follow, because it is hard for most of us to tell other people what their behavior

should look like—what we would see them doing if they reflected the qualities we are seeking.

For instance, you are much more likely to get results if you say, "*I* expect you to make at least three sales presentations per week" than you would by saying, "Why don't *you* quit wasting time around the office and go out and sign up some clients?"

Communicate as a Listener

So far, we have talked about situations in which you send or transmit messages. To be complete, however, communication also involves receiving information. The information you take in from others can be just as important as the information you send out. So listening is a very important skill to cultivate. Consider its impact through the following statistics:

We spend about 80 percent of our waking hours communicating, and most of that communicating involves listening. Between 40 percent and 80 percent of the typical professional salary is earned through listening. Yet most of us retain only 25 percent of what we hear forty-eight hours after we have heard it unless we write the information down.

Eighty percent of the people who fail in their jobs do so mainly because they cannot get along well with others. This failure is caused, at least in part, by poor listening—one of the major causes of misunderstandings between people. When management fails to listen properly, it also suffers. The best informational resource at management's disposal is its staff, and managers can shut down this resource simply by not listening to what their employees say.

Listening is a complex process. It consists of far more than simply hearing what is said. Listening also involves interpretation, evaluation, and reaction. This imposes responsibilities on listeners. Two basic listener responsibilities are:

- Making the communication process work efficiently and accurately.

- Making the speakers' messages do what they are intended to do.

To be a responsible listener, you will need to focus on the speaker. Remember that the message is not just in the words. It is in the speaker's eyes, facial expressions, tone, pitch, pace of voice, gestures, posture, and pauses—all the verbal and nonverbal cues that constitute the complete message.

Do not allow yourself to be distracted. Close your mind to the street noises outside, the conversation in the next cubicle, the pretty woman or the handsome man across the room. Do not let your thoughts wander toward what you are going to be doing that evening or where you are going on vacation. Give the speaker your total attention.

Do not try to seize the floor before the speaker is ready to yield it. Watch for door openers that allow you into the conversation. The speaker's body language often provides cues when it is your turn. A pause on the speaker's part also gives you a chance to respond without appearing to interrupt.

As you listen, put aside your own biases. Give the speaker a fair hearing. Suspend judgment on what is being said until you have had a chance to absorb the speaker's ideas and evaluate them. Do not interrupt the speaker, even to encourage. This can give the impression that you think you are more important than the speaker. Do not rehearse your response while the speaker is talking. When you do this, you are tuning out the speaker while you frame your reply, and you may be missing some important points.

A good listener anticipates instead of assuming. *Anticipation* means that you consider in advance what the speaker is likely to say and give it your consideration. *Assumption* means that you take for granted what is going to be said, accepting it arbitrarily or tentatively. The ability to anticipate helps you focus your attention on certain aspects of what the speaker is saying. Therefore, it helps you to remember certain information more effectively.

You anticipate on the basis of cues the speaker gives you within the context of the subject matter. On the basis of these cues, you "see" where the speaker is going. You anticipate with an open mind; you assume with a closed mind. If you decide, a few words into the presentation, that you already know everything the speaker is going to say, then you have made an assumption. Assumptions arise from your personal opinions, biases, and prejudices. You are most likely to make an assumption when you hear a speaker talk on a subject about which you already have strong feelings.

A good listener is sparing with questions. Wait for an indication that the speaker is ready to surrender the floor. Then ask your question. Do not pepper the speaker with pointed, specific questions as if you are a trial lawyer conducting a cross-examination. Use only a few well-chosen, open-ended questions that help elicit the speaker's message.

You can also use these occasions as opportunities to "bridge" to your own subject. When you are running out of time and need to convey some valuable information of your own, acknowledge what the speaker has said, make a transitional comment, then go into your message.

A good listener avoids giving advice—especially if it is unsolicited. Your objective in listening is to absorb the speaker's information, not to impart your own. Good listeners also avoid becoming defensive. Often, listeners read hidden intentions into a speaker's words. They expect to be attacked, and therefore go into a defensive posture. Some wait for the chance to attack, and listen intently for the points on which they can disagree. When you do that, you are ignoring the speaker's message and attempting to bend it toward your own ends.

Master silence. Use silence when you speak and when you listen. A pause gives both speaker and listener a chance to collect their thoughts. Neither should feel compelled to rush to fill the silent moment. Learn to be comfortable with silence. Often silence on the part of the listener opens the door to more information from the speaker. By sitting silently and expectantly, you encourage the speaker to think a moment, then resume speaking.

Reflective Listening

Reflective listening helps assure precision in communication. Reflective listeners give speakers feedback by paraphrasing what they have heard and repeating it in a clear and concise way until the speaker agrees, "Yes, that's what I meant." This demonstrates that the listener has been following the speaker. It clarifies meanings and generates understanding. It also causes the speaker to feel understood and "listened to."

If you do not understand the speaker's message, ask for clarification. As you receive messages, identify with the message-givers. Try to understand their problems and be responsive to them.

Sometimes we tend to concentrate on facts and shut out feelings. When we do, we miss out on a lot of important information. It is hard to understand the real meaning of what is being said without knowing something about the emotions that lie behind the words. Encourage others to share their feelings with you. As others share their feelings, accept them without passing judgment. Recognize that you can affect only the content of the message; you rarely can affect the feelings behind it. Understand, too, that feelings are transitory. Negative emotions are simply occupying a gap between more rational feelings. Wait, and these irrational responses will usually pass.

As you listen, demonstrate involvement in the conversation through your body language. Maintain good eye contact. Nod when the other person makes a point. Look for ways to indicate your positive interest in the speaker.

You can also indicate your sensitivity to the speaker's feelings through indirect means, such as your tone of voice and choice of words. Be careful to avoid overt identification with the speaker. When you say, "I know just how you feel," you are shifting the focus to yourself and indicating self-interest rather than interest in the other person. Be firm and compassionate in your responses, but make them relate to the points the speaker has made.

Finally, demonstrate your involvement through "physical listening." Lean toward the speaker. Face the speaker squarely and at eye level. Keep arms and legs uncrossed. Maintain an appropriate distance and avoid environmental distractions. Do not jangle keys, fiddle with earrings, or tug at your hair.

Power Communications by Telephone

Many of our everyday communications do not occur face to face. A dramatic example of this fact involves telephone communication. The telephone is an important mode of communication for all executives. It offers a challenge, because telephone dialogues require that you make your impression by voice alone, although you do communicate some body language with your voice. You can usually tell when the person on the other end of the telephone line is smiling and you can often visualize the posture of that person.

A client of mine—the president of two very large public employee associations—discovered this reality during a telephone interview with a radio station. He called me to tell me about it. "You'll never believe what I just did," he began. "I was in my office alone, the doors were closed, and I was working at my desk. My secretary told me I had a telephone call from an all-news radio station. And that's when it happened. Before I picked up the telephone, I stood up. I participated in the entire interview standing up."

As his media consultant, I asked him how he felt and sounded during the interview.

"Positive and authoritative," he responded.

I asked him how he might have done the interview before our consultations.

"I would have leaned back in my chair, propped my feet on the desk, and answered the questions," he said.

"And that's exactly how it would have sounded to the listeners," I reminded him.

Even though people cannot see you, they form an image of you through clues conveyed by your voice. So if you want to communicate with power, observe all the nuances of body language that you would observe if speaking face to face. When you are standing and holding the telephone at a natural angle, you communicate with more power. When you are seated, with the telephone jammed between shoulder and ear, your neck and head are in a strained position and you convey the strain through your voice box.

When you answer the telephone and begin your side of the conversation, use a rising inflection. This tells the caller that you are happy to receive the call. Speak softly. Nobody likes a voice that forces you to hold the telephone six inches from your ear. Besides, when you start softly, it leaves you room to raise your volume to emphasize the points you want to emphasize. Refer to your caller by name. Say the name slowly and clearly. As you identify yourself, pronounce your own name slowly and distinctly.

Effective telephone communication is a skill that you can learn and perfect through practice. Pay attention to the way you communicate by telephone, and regularly critique yourself. Notice people who are effective in telephone communication, and use them as positive role models.

As with any form of communication, it pays to start with a positive attitude. Adopt a voice and manner that say to the person on the other end of the line, "I am in charge. I can handle whatever problem comes my way." When you want something from the person on the other end, do not hesitate to make it known. Ask assertively.

As you listen to the other person, be alert for nuances. That person's voice is conveying subtle messages as well. Ask questions. If you are the recipient of the call, get a clear picture of the purpose of the call. Know what is expected of you and be prepared to deal with requests and demands.

If you are making the call, prepare yourself before you dial the number. Know what you want to accomplish and decide how you want to accomplish it. Be prepared, though, to offer the other party alternatives and options.

Some aspects of telephone manners represent basic courtesy. Answer the telephone promptly. Avoid putting people on hold unnecessarily, and when you do, minimize the hold time. Ask your callers whether they mind holding. Treat every caller with the same time consideration you would give to a person calling from a cellular telephone.

Evaluate your style to make sure that you speak conversationally. Monitor your voice tone and assess your voice quality.

Ending a telephone conversation requires forethought and planning. Always try for a smooth transition. You want the other party to feel that the conversation has come to a natural conclusion. So make time for the transition. Do not hesitate to bring the conversation to a close. Hesitation creates awkwardness. Be professional, pleasant, and firm as you conclude. Follow these steps to a graceful conclusion:

- Summarize the conversation and focus on conclusions you have reached.

- Review what needs to be done. Define each person's responsibilities.

- Conclude by acknowledging the importance of time to the other person.

- Let the other party hang up first. This will help ensure that the other party is ready to end the call.

Nobody's Perfect

Even when you have carried out all the suggestions in this chapter to the letter, you are going to make mistakes. Every communication process involves the transfer of information from one mind to another, and the information must pass through a unique set of filters in the sending mind and the receiving mind. That leaves plenty of room for garbled messages.

When mistakes do happen, deal with them in a professional way. First, accept the fact that mistakes are a part of life. The people who do not make mistakes are the people who do nothing. Accept responsibility for your own mistakes. Sure, others may have contributed to them. Your boss may have overloaded you with work, your subordinates may have undermined you, and an unreasonable client may have goaded you into an intemperate remark; but it was your decision to act or to react the way you did. Blaming others will not help solve your problem.

Release your mistakes emotionally. Do not wallow in guilt because you fouled up. Guilt robs you of energy and magnifies the damage done by a mistake. Put the mistake in the past, and move on. Regard mistakes as learning experiences. Analyze what went wrong and why it went wrong. Determine what you might have done differently to obtain a better result. Look for things you can do to avoid the mistake in the future.

Learn to laugh at mistakes. The ability to laugh at oneself is a valuable asset for a leader. Use your mistakes to build greater understanding of others who make mistakes. If you can forgive yourself for your own errors, you can also forgive others for theirs.

In Summary:

- Success in business is 85 percent dependent on effective communication and interpersonal skills.

- About 93 percent of your communication is nonverbal. You can learn to send powerful messages with the eyes, through facial expressions and voice qualities, through gestures, posture, and attire.

- You can communicate aggressiveness, submissive-ness, or assertiveness. Aggressiveness manipulates people and puts them on the defensive. Submissive-ness invites others to take advantage of you. Asser-tiveness involves open and honest communication in which you let others know clearly and tactfully what you desire from them.

- Listening is an important part of communication. By cultivating good listening skills, you open your-self to valuable information from others and put yourself in a better position to convey your own information.

- Telephone communication offers special challenges because you must convey your entire meaning by voice. Body language and posture, however, affect your voice quality and thus are indirectly conveyed by telephone.

- In terminating a telephone conversation, summarize what you have discussed, focusing on conclusions. Review the steps that need to be taken, reiterating the other party's responsibilities. Acknowledge the importance of time and let the caller know that it is okay to hang up. Let the other party hang up first.

- Since communication is necessarily imprecise, expect mistakes, accept them, learn from them, leave them in the past, and move on.

3

Communicating with High-Impact Words

The English language is a treasury of power-laden words. Think of the power of the Declaration of Independence to put steel into the resolve of the American colonies through its bold statement that "these united colonies are, and of right ought to be, free and independent states."

Consider the impact of Franklin Roosevelt's words to reassure a nation that was mired in depression and sliding toward war: "I pledge you, I pledge myself, to a new deal for the American people." And: "The only thing we have to fear is fear itself."

Reflect on the word power wielded by Winston Churchill as he rallied his beleaguered nation to confront the threat of a Germany that stood as the master of Europe:

> **Let us ... brace ourselves to our duties, and so bear ourselves that if the British Empire and its Commonwealth last for a thousand years, men will still say: "This was their finest hour."**

No wonder it was said of Churchill that he marshaled the English language and sent it marching to war. And no wonder he considered it an immense advantage that, as a student, "I got into my bones the essential structure of the ordinary British sentence—which is a noble thing." Few people can speak in any language with the eloquence of a Churchill, but all of us can learn to put energy into our speech. We can all learn to choose words that convey thoughts and emotions with power and precision.

Our Dual Linguistic Heritage

We who speak English have the advantage of a language that draws on a dual heritage. Our vocabulary is drawn from the Germanic tongue of the Anglo-Saxons and from the Latin foundation of their Norman French conquerors.

In addition, we have borrowed words from Greek and have absorbed others from the medley of languages that have added brilliant colors to the American mosaic or have been spoken under the British flag. Spanish, Italian, Yiddish, Arabic, Chinese, Japanese, and several Native American and African languages are among the assortment of tongues that have contributed to our store of words. For instance, the common expression "so long," meaning "good-bye," comes to us from the Arabic "salaam," which is akin to the Hebrew "Shalom"—words meaning "peace," and used in greeting people and in sending them on their way. By the time Moslem culture had spread it to Malaya, it had evolved into "Salang." The British picked it up there and brought it home as "so long."

If you look through your dictionary and count words, you will find that those of Latin origin outnumber those of Anglo-Saxon origin. But if you listen to everyday speech, you will find that the Anglo-Saxon language predominates. Anglo-Saxon words are usually shorter and punchier. The longer Latin words are often considered more elegant or more scholarly.

Even after the French and Anglo-Saxon languages had blended over the centuries into modern English, the Latin-based words maintained their aura of refinement, while the Anglo-Saxon words were often associated with coarse and vulgar things.

When Larry L. King's *The Best Little Whorehouse in Texas* was made into a movie, many newspapers refused to carry advertisements that featured the unexpurgated title. When you change the word "whorehouse" to "house of prostitution," you elevate it to the level of polite conversation, though you are still describing a house of ill repute. Remember that most people are more familiar with shorter words and descriptions.

Often long, multisyllabic words get in the way of the intended message. Consider this sentence, for instance: *Perspiring copiously, the intrepid vagabonds endeavored to surmount the precipice*. This sentence will quickly turn off most audiences. If you want to tell that story to a general audience, draw on your get-to-the-point vocabulary: *Sweating heavily, the fearless wanderers tried to climb the cliff.*

Short words provide a greater opportunity to be forceful and energetic. If you look back over Churchill's words that roused the British to the challenge of World War II, you will find that he effectively used a few relatively short words—*brace, duties,* and *finest.* On the other hand, sometimes longer words lend elegance and quiet strength to your language.

Positive, High-Impact Words

There are dozens of words that will boost your credibility. Here are just a few positive-impact words: *advantage, deserve, easy, guarantee, health, love, modern, money, positive, quality, safety, success, value,* and *you.*

You can also put your imprint on your position with a personal stand. Say "I want" instead of "many people want."

Be careful about using absolute words and phrases. The word *all* is an absolute word that can have high impact. Other words that require precise usage are: *every, none, only, unique, best, worst, first,* and *final.* These words do not equivocate. Just be sure that you use them only when appropriate. Remember, you are accountable for what you say.

When the United States Supreme Court decreed an end to segregated schools, it called for desegregation to proceed, not with "deliberate speed" but "with *all* deliberate speed." Abraham Lincoln did not call upon the shattered nation to pull itself together "with malice toward few, with charity for most." It was "with malice toward *none*, with charity for *all*."

Franklin Roosevelt did not say, "One of the few things we have to fear is fear itself." He said, "The *only* thing we have to fear is fear itself."

Avoid "Vocal Disclaimers"

As a speaker, you might unknowingly pull your punches by using "vocal disclaimers" or "softeners"— words that equivocate or that qualify the statement you are making. Unfortunately, these words and phrases alert the listener that what you are about to say has questionable credibility; even worse, the listener might develop doubts about you and your ability to speak credibly about the subject.

Suppose Patrick Henry had said, "Give me liberty or give me death, *so to speak*." Or suppose Winston Churchill had said, "*As far as I know,* I have nothing to offer but blood, toil, tears, and sweat." Or suppose Thomas Jefferson had written, "*In our opinion,* all men are created equal."

Note how these softeners rob the statements of their ring and power. Other common vocal disclaimers are:

- It seems to me . . .

- I think . . .

- I could be mistaken, but . . .

- I'll double-check my facts, but . . .

- Is it me, or did I observe . . . ?

- I know you might interpret this as . . .

- Time may prove me wrong, of course, but . . .

- It is the judgment of many, including me . . .

- I feel . . .

- I guess . . .

- I believe . . .

Of course, the ideal way to handle information is to be able to make statements of fact. However, we do not always have all the facts when we are required to share information publicly. Rather than jeopardize your credibility with vocal disclaimers, therefore, you can soften a statement by using such words as *might, could, should, would, must, possibly,* and *probably.* For example, a statement of fact would be "It is going to rain today." With a vocal disclaimer the statement could be "*I think* it is going to rain today." To maintain your credibility while softening the statement you could say, "It *might* rain today" or "It *must* rain today." Notice that the word softener you choose will have a direct impact on the meaning and force of your message.

One exception to this vocal disclaimer rule is followed by high-profile political leaders. Often they intentionally use vocal disclaimers when speaking about difficult issues. By softening their statements they are able to humble themselves to their audiences in efforts to gain support.

You will also want to avoid "vocal detours"—the sounds that interrupt or intrude into fluent speech. Common detours are *uh, er, well, okay,* and *you know.* These detours usually result from a fear of momentary silence. Not only is it okay, it is also effective to remain silent, or pause, while you think of your next sentence. Train yourself to listen for these detours. See how long you can go without using them. Soon, you will clear them out of your speech.

Avoid Jargon and Euphemisms

Every vocation has its own private language—terms that are understood by those within the vocational group but are not so familiar to those on the outside. Some people like to use this jargon because they think these expressions give them a special aura of expertise or of specialized knowledge. Quite often, they tend to turn people off.

Let me demonstrate my point. Following a seminar I once gave on public personhood, an attorney approached me with a concerned look on his face. He told me that he disagreed with my recommendation that public persons use short, understandable words when possible. He had been raised in a rural community and wanted to impress judges that he was well educated. So he chose to use multisyllabic words, many of them steeped in excessive legal jargon. I told him that the words he used to impress the judges would be the same words he would need to impress the juries.

The world of politics is full of jargon, also known as bureaucratese. Warren Harding is blamed for taking us away from normality and into *normalcy*. During the Eisenhower administration, we stopped completing things and began *finalizing* them. In the early sixties political leaders stopped thinking and started having *judgments,* as in "My opponent, in my judgment, is an irresponsible, vacillating prevaricator." During the Watergate hearings, events stopped happening now and then and began happening *at this point in time* and *at that point in time.*

Bureaucracies in business are also overburdened with jargon. Avoid it. Do not *conceptualize* when you can *imagine*; do not *guesstimate* when you can make a *rough estimate*; do not *implement* when you can *carry out*; do not *interface* when you can *talk with.* Also avoid turning nouns and adjectives into verbs by appending *-ize,* such as *normalize* and *actualize.*

And do not use abbreviations or acronyms unless you are confident that your audience is familiar with them. Most Americans are more familiar with the acronyms *NATO* and *NASA* than they are with the words they represent. But do not use *BUPERS* unless you are addressing a Naval audience that will readily understand you to mean "Bureau of Naval Personnel." And do not use *BWC* unless you are speaking on the campus of a school that is a member of the Big West Conference.

You also blunt the impact of your words when you use euphemisms. A euphemism, according to Webster's, is a word or phrase that is "less expressive or direct, but considered less distasteful, less offensive, than another."

The trouble with most euphemisms is that people tend to know when you are using them, and they feel that you are trying to put something over on them. When you refer to an instrument for manual excavation, people know you mean a shovel, and they would think more highly of you if you called it a shovel. Likewise, as corporate speech writer Joan Detz reminds us, there is no use disguising a test as a *classification device*, a group as an *interrelated collectivity*, or laziness as *motivational deprivation*.[1] Show your respect for your audience by expressing your ideas boldly and openly. The audience will reciprocate by respecting you.

Your language is also weakened when you use vague words that convey little or no information. *Various* is one of the most common of these words. When you say, "I am proud of my various accomplishments," you are using one word too many. Drop the word *various* and your listener is just as well informed. Modifiers such as *very, slightly, extremely, quite,* and *rather* are impact-robbers. *Several* and *many* rarely help convey strong meaning. Specific quantities are preferable. And when you say "*scores* of people," be aware that a score really means twenty. *Myriads,* often used to indicate a large but indefinite number, literally means "tens of thousands." When possible, be specific. Speaking of literally, be careful how you use this word. When you say something like "I *literally* died," you are saying that you actually died; if you use the word literally, make sure that you mean it.

Use Active Voice and Repetition for Impact

Your language is more forceful when you choose the active voice over the passive. The active voice means that the subject is *performing* the action rather than being the object of the action. You use the passive voice when you say, "Desert Storm was won by the United States and its allies over Iraq." You use the active voice when you say, "The United States and its allies defeated Iraq in Desert Storm." Active sentences transmit more power. Let them predominate in your spoken and written communications.

Repetition can be a pile driver pounding home the impact of your words. Consider Admiral William "Bull" Halsey's formula for victory: "Hit hard, hit fast, and hit often." Consider Abraham Lincoln's classic "of the people, by the people, and for the people." A coach can multiply the force of his words by telling his team, "It takes three things to win: play hard, play hard, and play hard."

Semantic Baggage

Some words carry overtones beyond their literal meanings. These overtones may be temporary, depending upon political and social events. They may be subtle or flagrant. We call this *semantic baggage.*

For instance, during the heyday of the Union of Soviet Socialist Republics, the term *Soviet Union* lent a respectability to the communist system while the term *Russia* implied that the "union" was really an empire of provinces subjugated and dominated by Russia. Similarly, the term *Communist China* usually carries a pejorative meaning, while *The People's Republic of China* conveys an aura of respectability. *Mainland China* is a safe, neutral term. *The West Bank* is a politically neutral term for the territory that Israel captured from Jordan in the Six Day War of 1967. Those who refer to it as *Judea* and *Samaria* are saying, through their choice of terms, that this territory is historically a part of Israel and should remain so in the future.

When someone refers to Native Americans, you can infer that the speaker's politics are left of center. A conservative would likely say American Indians.

Maintaining Gender Neutrality

In this age of expanding rights for women and minorities, keeping your language gender-neutral is a constant challenge. Our Anglo-Saxon predecessors did not make it easy for us. Their language did not contain a gender-neutral third-person singular pronoun that could refer to a person. They gave us *he, his,* and *him* for males, *she, her,* and *hers* for females, and *it* and *its* for things without gender. But if you are referring to a group of males and females, if you are referring to one gender or the other, or if you are not sure about the gender, you are up a creek. Some people resort to using *he* or *she* or, in writing, *he/she.* This is awkward and distracting. Others opt for a plural pronoun, even though the antecedent may be singular. This is a popular device in everyday speech, but it offends those who insist on correct grammar. Let's look at some ways these situations can be handled.

Consider this sentence: *If a speaker wants to communicate effectively, he or she must choose his or her words carefully.* Obviously, that is an awkward and unnatural way of making your statement. Grammarians historically have held that in such instances the masculine pronoun can serve both genders. But nowadays, many listeners—both men and women—consider this sexist. Fortunately, a couple of devices can be used to make it gender-neutral and natural-sounding. One is to resort to the plural. When you do this, be sure that the pronoun and its antecedent are both plural. Thus, you could rephrase it this way: *Speakers who want to communicate effectively must choose their words carefully.*

The other device is to shift to the second person, as in this version: *If you want to communicate effectively, you must choose your words carefully.*

Some of the most difficult cases to handle involve the use of pronouns that appear to be plural but actually are singular. When you use *each, every, everyone,* or *everybody,* you are talking about more than one person, but you are thinking about them one person at a time. Thus, grammarians have historically thought of these words as singular. Even when you speak of *anyone* or *anybody,* you are often thinking of more than one person, but you are thinking of them one person at a time.

The problem occurs when you need a second pronoun as an antecedent to these pronouns. Consider this sentence: *Anyone who wants to impress an audience must watch his/her language.* The old-style grammarian would tell you that it is correct to say, "Anyone . . . must watch *his* language." But that wording will leave many listeners with the impression that you are insensitive to women. Most casual speakers would say, "Anyone . . . must watch *their* language," but English purists would cringe at this use of a plural pronoun with a singular antecedent.

Here again, it is best to rephrase, using the gender-neutral plural or second person to get around the awkward situation. Here are three possible rephrasings:

1. *All who want to impress their audiences must watch their language.*

2. *Those who want to impress their audience must watch their language.*

3. *If you want to impress an audience, you must watch your language.*

With a little effort and ingenuity, you can avoid the *his/her* awkwardness in almost every case without abandoning gender neutrality. If you cannot find a way to avoid *his/her,* be even-handed about it. You can alternate between *his/her* and *her/his.* Or, like some authors and speakers, you can alternate between *his* and *her.* Your audiences will appreciate your impartiality.

Since gender neutrality is a fairly new concept in English, our language is loaded with nouns that seem to apply to only one gender. We have grown accustomed to speaking of businessmen as though women never went into business; of foremen as if women never supervised others; of chairman as though women have never held leadership positions with committees and organizations.

Increasingly, though, sensitive writers and speakers are finding gender-neutral substitutes for such sex-specific terms. If you refer to a woman as a *spokesman,* many of your listeners will try to raise your consciousness. The Associated Press prefers *spokeswoman,* although many people would prefer the gender-neutral *spokesperson.* If you do not know whether the spokesperson is male or female, AP recommends that you use *representative.* It is easy enough to say *businessperson* instead of *businessman. Firemen* become *firefighters, policemen* become *police officers, workmen* become *workers, manpower* becomes *work force, congressmen* become *members of Congress,* and *mankind* becomes *human beings.* If you do not want a *waiter* or a *waitress* to bring you your steak and cannot quite bring yourself to say *waitperson,* order it from a *server.* With a little practice, you can make gender-neutral terms a natural part of your vocabulary.

Know What You're Saying

Skilled communicators learn to use words with precision, which means that they must be aware of precise meanings.

Some words are spoken out of both corners of the mouth. *Presently,* for instance, can mean either *now* or *soon.* If you say, "Presently, I'm serving as chairman of the Ways and Means Committee," you could mean that you currently are holding that position, which is the popular use of the word; or that you expect to hold the position shortly, which is the grammarian-sanctioned meaning. Usually, the context tells the listener which meaning you have in mind, but it is better to use a word that has only one clear meaning. You can say *"Currently,* I'm serving . . ."* and your listener will have no doubt as to your meaning. Or you can take advantage of Anglo-Saxon terseness and say "I'm *now* serving," or—if you want to be even more succinct—simply "I'm serving." If you are using *presently* in its future sense, of course, it is simple to say "Soon I will serve."

The word *unique* has been misused so often that it has almost lost its unique meaning. Many speakers and writers use it to mean *unusual,* and they often try to strengthen it by calling something *most unique* or *very unique.* Its true meaning is "one of a kind." If there is anything else like it, it is not unique. Therefore, a thing is either unique or it is not unique. It cannot be *most* unique or *very* unique, and one thing cannot be more unique than another.

The word *infer* is often used when the intended meaning is *imply.* To *infer* is to derive by reasoning; to draw a conclusion. To *imply* is to indicate, without saying openly or directly. If I say that I am thinking of buying a new Rolls Royce, I am *implying* that I am quite affluent. You may *infer* that I am wealthy. Remember that the speaker implies, while the listener infers.

Comprise is another frequently misused word. Many speakers use it as a synonym for *compose,* as in "The United States is *comprised* of fifty states and the District of Columbia." Actually, it is synonymous with *include,* as in "The United States *comprises* fifty states and the District of Columbia." If you say *comprised of,* you are using the word incorrectly. Use *composed of* or *made up of* when that is what you mean. In most cases in which *comprise* is the proper word, you will be understood more clearly if you say *include*.

Some other words are more often misused in the written than in the spoken language. There are subtle differences in spelling and pronunciation between *forebear* and *forbear*, and between *foregoing* and *forgoing*, but the differences in meaning are not subtle. *Forebear* is a noun meaning an ancestor. *Forbear* is a verb meaning "to restrain" or "to abstain." If you discover that Thomas Jefferson is a *forebear* of yours, you may not be able to *forbear* telling others about it. To *forego* is to go ahead of. To *forgo* is to do without. *Constrain* is a word less frequently used, and with good reason. It has two meanings which are almost the opposite of each other. To *constrain* can mean to *urge* forcibly or to *restrain* forcibly. If there is a possibility of confusion, do not use it.

Another potentially confusing word pair is *ingenious* and *ingenuous*. *Ingenious* means clever, as in "The lapel mike was an ingenious invention." *Ingenuous* means "candid." We encounter it most often in its negative form, *disingenuous*, which means "less than candid" or "deceptive." *Disingenuous* can be a euphemism for "lying."

If someone tells you that you are about to enjoy the *penultimate* experience, call the police or call a doctor. *Penultimate* does not mean "beyond the ultimate." It means "next to last," and if the experience that is coming up is to be your next to last one, you are in deep trouble.

It is good to expand your vocabulary by picking up a new word every day. You may do this by singling out an unfamiliar word in your daily reading materials and looking it up in the dictionary. Or you may simply comb the dictionary for new and unusual words. Before you use them yourself, however, try to find several places where others have used them. Sometimes the dictionary gives examples of usage. You may also find it helpful to look up a word in dictionaries of quotations, such as Bartlett's *Familiar Quotations.*

Observing the way others use words helps you to use them in the proper context, with the proper meanings. Never use a word—in speaking or writing—when you are unsure of the precise meaning. A speaker once told a group that his organization would try to land the vice president of the United States as a speaker at its conference, "but he doesn't look too promiscuous." The speaker thought he had found a fancy way to say "promising," when he was actually saying "sexually active." Before you use a fancy word, ask yourself whether you can communicate more effectively with a simple, well-understood word. If the fancy word is still your choice, use it—but only after you have looked it up.

In Summary:

- The English language is enriched by its dual Latin-Germanic heritage and by the infusion of words from many languages via the British Empire and the American mosaic.

- In the dictionary, Latin words, which tend to be more elegant, outnumber Anglo-Saxon words, which are usually softer and more energetic. However, Anglo-Saxon predominates in everyday speech.

- All things being equal, the shorter, more common word is preferable to the longer, less common word.

- Some positive, high-impact words that serve speakers well are *advantage, discover, easy, guarantee, health, love, money, new, positive, proven, results, safety, save,* and *you.*

- Avoid vocal disclaimers that soften the impact of your message.

- Avoid euphemisms, jargon, words that have vague meanings, and words that have ambiguous meanings.

- Speakers and writers should be cognizant of words that carry semantic baggage and use them only when they are aware of the words' literal meanings and overtones.

- Speakers and writers should maintain gender neutrality. Two devices for avoiding the use of sexist pronouns when referring to both sexes or either sex are to shift to the gender-neutral plural number or to use the second person.

- Be familiar with the precise meanings of words and brush up on the meanings of words that are commonly misused.

- Never use an unfamiliar word until you have looked it up in the dictionary and have seen or heard it used in context by a knowledgeable speaker or writer.

Notes

1. Joan Detz, *How to Write and Give a Speech* (New York: St. Martin's Press, 1984), 54.

4

Responsibilities of a Public Person

To position yourself as an influential leader, it is important for you to recognize the impact you have as a public person. Public persons are people who are known or recognized by many people they themselves do not know. Public persons can acquire this status through *birth, choice, circumstance,* or a combination of all three. For the remainder of this book I will focus on positive public personhood that directly or indirectly benefits the individual and the community. You can define your community geographically, professionally, economically, and in many other ways.

Most of us enjoy walking down Main Street in our hometowns and exchanging greetings with people we know and like. It is quite another experience when people you do not know see you, call you by name, and congratulate you for something you have accomplished.

When you are a public person, your identity lends an attention-getting quality to your name. Ralph Nader is a public person. What he says about consumer affairs gets attention in the media across the land.

Lee Iacocca is a public person. His highly recognizable face and style helped him significantly when he led Chrysler back from the brink of bankruptcy. People still listen to him when he talks about business management.

Michael Jordan is a public person. His name is a sought-after commodity among those who want to sell athletic shoes, hamburgers, soft drinks, and other items.

You do not have to be a superstar in athletics, business, consumer advocacy, or anything else to be a public person. Every community, large or small, has its public persons who are known throughout the community for who they are and what they do.

We learned in chapter 1 that community involvement provides a powerful avenue toward leadership and recognition. To achieve a position of recognition and esteem in your community, you will need to cultivate the qualities of a public person.

Leadership imposes responsibility. Once you have asked people to follow you, you accept a major responsibility for results. Public persons accept this responsibility, knowing that it also poses risks. If you fail to accomplish your objective, the people who followed you are likely to hold you accountable. The truth is, of course, that if nobody leads, nothing gets accomplished, and it is better to have tried and failed than to have failed by not trying.

Yet, as a public person, you must not let failure defeat you. True leaders regard failure as a prelude to success. They learn from their failures and use their new knowledge to help them lead others toward success.

Leadership compensates for the risks by conferring power and privileges upon those who accept the responsibility. People seek out successful leaders for advice and look to them for influence. The more successfully you develop your leadership, the greater your influence and power. When you take the role of a leader and public person in business, your recognized status acts as a magnet to draw toward you the people who can help you in your business. Put simply, your good name takes on a profit-generating power.

Your First Responsibility: Know Yourself

Public persons need keen insights into others. The process starts, of course, with a keen insight into yourself. What makes you tick? What are your capacities? What are your limitations? Not everyone has the capacity to perform microsurgery. Not everyone can pilot a shuttle craft. Not everyone has the talent to compose a great piano concerto. But each of us is good at *something*. Use your self-knowledge to discover something that you perform or know well and that you enjoy doing. When you are good at something that you enjoy, you have two powerful sources of motivation. Your enjoyment of the task leads you to work at it long and persistently. By working long and skillfully at the task, you achieve successes. Each success adds to your pleasure, which motivates you to work even harder and, therefore, enhances your expertise.

Successful people do not work long and hard because they are driven. They work long and hard because they enjoy what they are doing. They enjoy meeting challenges and overcoming them. To add that kind of motivation to your life, first you will need to determine what you want to achieve. Get in touch with your basic values and ask yourself simply, "What do I want?"

Once you have made that basic determination, set realistic, achievable goals that will lead you toward your ultimate desire. Set timetables, and begin working purposefully toward these goals. As you successfully achieve them, stop and celebrate. When you do not reach your objectives, ask yourself why. Turn that message into a learning experience. What you have learned from this failure will help you build toward your ultimate success.

Living and Succeeding in a World of Stress

Public people live in a world of stress. Many people regard stress-borne illnesses, such as ulcers and cardiovascular ailments, as the price you must pay for success. But stress does not have to be the mother of illness. It can be the mother of accomplishment—and of happiness.

People who go through life avoiding stress do not lead fulfilling existences. Stress prepares us for challenges. If you are not challenged, you will not achieve. The unchallenged person vegetates. Competition is a form of healthy stress. The communist states manufactured products of poor quality because their products were not subjected to the competition of the marketplace. Without competition, people had no incentive to make things better. The only arena in which communist-bloc products approached Western products in quality was in the military field, where the communists consciously competed with the West.

Imagine what might have happened in the automotive industry had no one competed with Henry Ford to mass-produce automobiles. Automakers would have had no incentive to streamline the Model T, provide it with a self-starter, an enclosed body, a more powerful engine, a softer ride, a radio, heater, air conditioning, automatic transmission, power steering— all the things that have made the modern automobile comfortable, reliable, and fun to drive.

Just as the stress of competition hones the quality of manufactured products, so it can hone the quality of the individual. The stress of challenge motivates us to meet the challenge. In meeting that challenge, we acquire experience, expertise, confidence, and the motivation to meet and master new challenges.

Stress, therefore, is not something you need to avoid; rather, it is something you can manage and utilize. It is not the enemy; in fact, it is the body's mechanism for dealing successfully with enemies. In humankind's primitive state, the enemy might have been a bear, a lion, or a wolf pack. In modern times, the "enemy" more often takes the form of everyday challenges that stand between us and the things we want to achieve.

A team of athletes going into a big game feels stress. They can allow this stress to become a negative force. The players can spend the day of the contest worrying about the other team and fretting over the possibility that when the big moment comes, they will not measure up. If these players succumb to this stress, they will probably lose. However, they have the choice to turn stress into a positive force by imagining themselves performing superbly on the field. The athletes can picture themselves executing each play perfectly and savor the thrill of victory in advance. This positive approach will enable the team members to take the field with self-confidence and let their stress energize them to perform their best.

The same thing can happen if you are a salesperson preparing for a big presentation. You can subject yourself to negative stress by worrying about losing the sale. Or you can make use of positive stress by mentally rehearsing your presentation and imagining the things you can do with the proceeds from the sale.

Chronic Stress

No matter how positively we look at challenges, no matter how optimistically we pursue our mental rehearsals, things do not always go the way we want them to go. You give your sales presentation perfectly, but the prospect turns you down. The new boss comes in determined to shake up the organization, and the innovative ideas you have diligently worked on are discarded like the day's trash. You may even become the victim of a layoff. Or perhaps an economic downturn strikes just as you are trying to get your business off the ground. The business climate is changing, and you do not know where these changes are leading or how they will affect you.

Change generates stress. Any change in the status quo—whether good or bad—upsets the equilibrium and introduces stress. The stress remains until the equilibrium is restored—until your mind and body have adjusted to the new realities. If these changes come so fast that you are unable to adjust to them, you may fall victim to chronic stress. This kind of stress can lead to serious illness.

Fortunately, you can learn how to cope with this kind of stress. Often, chronic stress arises from repeated rejection or repeated failure. Successful salespeople know that they will be rejected regularly. They will not make a sale each time they make a presentation. So they learn to accept each rejection, knowing that if they persevere, they eventually will make a sale. They analyze each rejection and use what they learn to build toward the next success.

The same can prove true with any enterprise. Few inventions worked on the first try. Thomas Edison logged hundreds of failures before he invented the electric light. Every failure had a purpose and made a contribution to his eventual success. If you find yourself succumbing to stress, do not surrender. You can take positive steps to deal with it. For example:

- **Measure the problem.** How important is it? We often waste our time fretting over minor things that amount to little in the overall scheme. If it is of minor consequence, accept it as a normal part of living and do not let it bother you.

- **Do something about it.** If you cannot live with the problem comfortably, make a conscious decision to do something about it. Then go to work promptly to execute your decision. You may have to confront the person who is causing you stress. You may have to change your physical location, buy additional equipment, or change your normal routine. Whatever you have to do, *do* it.

- **Learn when to walk away.** Sometimes you may find yourself fighting hopeless battles. You hate your job, you cannot stand your boss, and you see no prospect for things getting better. Do not keep butting your head against a stone wall. Find another job and another boss with whom you are more compatible.

- **Put the stress to work.** Look for ways in which the stress can help you grow. Tell yourself that you can emerge from the situation as a better person, and take steps to fulfill that promise.

- **Talk about it.** Find someone you trust and feel close to and share your problem. "Talking it out" often helps you to put things in perspective and sort out your options. It is also a good tension-reliever.

- **Give yourself credit.** When your self-esteem is taking a beating, stop and remind yourself of all the positive assets you have and all the good things you have accomplished. When you confront a stressful event and overcome it, congratulate yourself. This will give you the confidence to face the next stressful event.

You have other options to minimize stress in your daily life. Seek variety. If you do the same thing every day, with no change of pace, tension builds up. Find a hobby—preferably one that is not related to your occupational field. Seek out new interests. Treat yourself to a night out once in a while. Cultivate a circle of supportive friends and draw strength from them.

Exercising will also help you relieve stress. It need not be vigorous and demanding. A long, quiet walk at lunchtime can give you a chance to work off tension and relax the mind. Remember that good health habits will help you during times of stress. Do not try to relieve stress through smoking or drinking. Instead, maintain a balanced diet, get plenty of sleep, and get the proper exercise. The better physical shape you are in, the better you are prepared to cope with negative stress. Take time to relax. Listen to your body signals. When you feel yourself all tensed up, with your stomach in knots, your ears ringing, and your muscles taut, stop what you are doing. Concentrate. Take deep, steady breaths. Let your mind wander to some relaxing spot and put yourself there, enjoying the surroundings, free of worries.

Most public persons have thresholds of stress—points at which stress becomes bothersome or distressful to them. If you identify that threshold and determine in advance how you will deal with it, you will find yourself facing stressful situations with confidence—and that in itself will reduce the negative effects of the stress.

Cultivate a Positive Attitude

The public person must cultivate a positive attitude. Leadership is as much an art as it is a skill. It involves the ability to get other people involved in and committed to something you, as a leader, clearly recognize needs to be done. You do not become a leader by saying, "I'm going to lead." You do it by saying, "We need to get this done and I'm going to do it." You gather support along the way, and people naturally follow you. Why? Because you are the one who is providing positive direction.

Success is more than an outcome; it is an attitude. We achieve success because we recognize and appreciate who we are and what we have accomplished. We are able to look forward to what can be rather than look backward to what could have been. We develop a positive attitude when we determine to work with what we have, to expand it, to increase our knowledge, and to apply it toward specific objectives. Specific objectives give us positive motivation. If you are hiking and all you can see ahead of you is an uphill grade, you may eventually become discouraged.

"It's all uphill," you may say. "I'm never going to reach the top." But if you can catch sight of the summit toward which you are climbing, you can see a specific objective. You can measure your progress as you go. You can see how far you have come and compare it with the distance you have yet to travel. Seeing the summit drawing closer gives you an incentive to continue your climb. You now have a positive attitude.

You can strengthen that positive attitude by setting incremental goals along the way. You may see a large rock ahead and tell yourself, "When I reach that rock, I'm going to stop and rest a moment." You now have a positive goal that is within relatively easy reach. You may see a clump of trees still farther up the trail, and you may tell yourself, "When I reach that clump, I'll stop and have a snack." Again, you have a positive goal.

You can apply the same principle to goals in life. Your long-range goal may be to own your own company. Your incremental goals might be to acquire management experience in the company for which you work, to move into an executive position, and to accumulate capital for your own company. Set short-term goals that are realistic and reachable, map a plan for reaching them, and set out positively to execute the plan. When an obstacle blocks your path, do not look upon it as an impassable roadblock. View it as a minor barrier that you can negotiate, and never doubt that you will negotiate it.

Nurture a Sense of Humor

Public persons recognize that one of their most valuable assets is a sense of humor. "Laugh, and the world laughs with you," wrote Ella Wheeler Wilcox. "Weep, and you weep alone." If you can laugh at yourself, you have the potential to disarm your critics and attract many people to your side. If you soften your criticism with subtle humor, you can avoid inflicting wounds that shout for vengeance. If you laugh amid setbacks, you can lubricate the passage through adversity.

Winston Churchill had a legendary deadpan sense

of humor. After the Germans had driven the British from the continent and appeared poised for an invasion of England, Churchill told the French in a radio broadcast: "We are waiting for the long-promised invasion. So are the fishes."

Abraham Lincoln also considered humor a strong ally in times of trial. At one point, when he was chafing for action from the Union army while its commander, George McClellan, kept waiting for just the right moment to move, Lincoln observed: "It is called the Army of the Potomac, but it is only McClellan's bodyguard. . . . If McClellan is not using the army, I should like to borrow it for a while." On another occasion, when critics complained that General U. S. Grant was a heavy drinker, Lincoln reportedly responded, "Find out what kind of whiskey he drinks; I'd like to send some to my other generals."

John Kennedy could employ humor to humble himself and his audiences. Once, when addressing a White House dinner and reception honoring Nobel Prize winners, Kennedy observed: "I think this is the most extraordinary collection of talent, of human knowledge, that has ever been gathered together at the White House, with the possible exception of when Thomas Jefferson dined alone."

At another time when Kennedy was criticized for appointing his own brother Robert Kennedy as attorney general despite his lack of experience as a lawyer, the president responded playfully that "Bobby has to get his experience *somewhere.*"

The ability to laugh at yourself establishes you as a person with self-confidence. The ability to soften your blows with humor establishes you as a person of sensitivity. The ability to laugh amid adversity allows you to vent stress in a positive way and clear your mind and body for action. The public person needs such assets.

Everyone can learn to use humor effectively. You just want to make sure that you use discretion with humor. Here are some suggestions on how to create your own humor anthology:

- **Build a comedy collection.** Jot down any jokes, one-liners, or stories that you find funny. Practice saying them out loud and decide whether you are better at telling stories like Bill Cosby or spitting out one-liners like Jay Leno. Build on which style works best for you.

- **Do not wait.** Look for humor before you need to start writing your speech. You should always be on the lookout for humorous material in joke books, magazines, and elsewhere. However, remember that once material is published, the whole world has access to it; therefore, your best source of humor is you. Your acquaintances, your friends, and your aspirations can be some of the most dynamic sources for your stories. Be willing to reach as far back as your childhood for anecdotes.

- **"Own" your material.** Adapt it to your own style and put it into your own words. Do not do anything that would be out of character for you as a person or as an executive. Especially remember that you should not resort to off-color jokes or offensive or biased remarks in an attempt to endear yourself to your listeners.

- **Adapt your material to your audience.** If you use a caustic style of humor, be sure you know the audience and are confident the jocular insults will be taken well. For example, several years ago, I attended a leadership development program for eighty high-powered corporate leaders. Throughout the session the moderator gave transitional comments so that by lunchtime he felt very comfortable with the audience. Prior to introducing the luncheon speaker he remarked from his position at the podium, "Anyone who needs to use the telephones can find them across the hall, and by the way, for those of you who want to 'do your duty,' the bathrooms are across the hall, too." The response from the audience was one of shock and discomfort, and it took only a very brief moment for him to realize that he had mishandled his casual humor.

If you are uncertain about how your humor will be received, do not include it. You can often handle difficult or sensitive professional situations with humor. The following are six ways you can create humorous bridges between challenging circumstances and workable solutions:

1. *Focus your humor on the situation, not the person.* Remember that you want to find a resolution without destroying the members of your team. You do not want to single out people for mistakes when your intention is to correct a problem. So, if one of your staff has tipped over a glass of water and drenched your sales report, you could say, "No one told me our policy is to leave the windows open during torrential rains."

2. *Direct laughter at the problem, not at yourself.* By using self-directed humor you are able to humanize

the situation. However, be careful not to deprecate yourself. Your intention is to resolve the problem, not to put yourself down. So, if you forget to bring handouts to a board of directors meeting or public presentation, you could say, "I really messed up and came unprepared." Or you can use humor and say, "That's the last time I let the Invisible Man make copies for me."

3. *Remember perspective.* Often, during difficult times, we immerse ourselves in the minute details of our own professional problems, thus losing sight of the bigger picture. To help you take advantage of perspective, put time, distance, and good humor between you and your project. One of my father's favorite sayings is, "Don't worry about it. In sixty years you won't even remember it."

4. *Appreciate playfulness in other people.* When we internalize our careers, our professional responsibilities, and our day-to-day dilemmas, we sometimes overlook the value of lightheartedness in other people. A client who runs a financial management consulting company sent me a gift at the completion of one of our joint projects. It was distinctively gift-wrapped in paper for Valentine's Day, the Fourth of July, Halloween, and New Year's Day. The attached card read, "A special gift for the woman of all seasons."

5. *Nurture humor in your mind's eye.* Learn to visualize humor. Create humorous images in your mind, especially when you need to relieve yourself from stressful situations. This exercise can be as easy as remembering the last time you experienced a tear-producing laugh and what prompted you to laugh so hard. Or you can re-create a humorous scene from your favorite movie. Empower yourself to relive that

moment and how good it made you feel. For example, in the movie "City Slickers," Billy Crystal plays the part of a businessman who, along with his two best friends, travels all over the world to experience adventure. They decide to go on a cattle drive despite not even knowing how to mount a horse. In one scene, the head cattleman tells Crystal to lasso a calf. Crystal, in a self-confident way, says it's no problem, so he gets off his horse, walks over to the calf, and places the lasso over the calf's head. He then smirks at the cattleman, who smirks back and shoots his gun into the air, prompting the calf to run and thus drag Crystal behind. As he is bouncing about the landscape at full speed, Crystal looks into the camera and says, "And I'm on a vacation."

6. *Use humor as a powerful motivator.* The late Sam Walton, founder of WalMart Stores, once told his employees that if they would generate record profits for the fiscal year, he would dance the hula down Wall Street. When his employees met the challenge, Walton did indeed don a grass skirt and dance his way down Wall Street. Walton knew how to do business with a chuckle. He laughed all the way to the bank.

Dealing with Angry or Complaining People

The public person learns to deal with hostile complainers. Leaders know that criticism goes with the territory. Leadership means accepting responsibility, and that means responsibility for what goes right, as well as for what goes wrong.

Most people respond to criticism in the ways they learned as children. They go into a defensive posture, making excuses for whatever they have failed to do. They practice denial. Whatever was done or was not done, it was not their fault or their responsibility. They counterattack by striking back at their critics, thereby diverting attention from their own failures. Or they withdraw into helpless silence. Public persons learn to deal with criticism on an adult level. This enables them to grow as a result of criticism rather than being diminished by it.

The first important step to take when an angry critic confronts you is to try to understand the critic's motives. For some people, criticism is an effort to dominate more passive people and put themselves in command. Others use criticism as a manipulative device. They usually preface their complaints with "You never," hoping to use guilt as a means of getting their way. Another function of criticism is to inflict punishment. Sometimes, related to this, critics challenge listeners for things they do themselves and subconsciously relieve their own guilt by projecting it on others. Also, some critics confront people to make themselves feel bigger or get more attention.

Criticism can stem from positive motives, too. Constructive critiquing can help you become better at what you are doing. By taking a critical look, you can alert yourself to things you are doing that are harming a relationship. This analysis could help you communicate feelings or show compassion. Sometimes a strong critique can enable you to assert legitimate self-interest.

To determine the motive and analyze the criticism requires that you listen and observe. Silent observation can be a powerful aid in determining motives and in evaluating the validity of criticism. To practice it, you have to do something that can be difficult: refrain from responding to the criticism. Instead, take as long as you need to listen to all the criticism that is going on around you—criticism of others as well as criticism of yourself. This lets you look at criticism objectively.

As you listen to the criticism, ask yourself what motivation is behind it, how you feel about it, and whether your feelings are keeping you from making positive use of it. Is the criticism valid? If so, to what extent? Much of what you hear may be judgmental. If a critic says you are lazy, selfish, or greedy, you have learned nothing except the critic's current opinion of you. Listen for words that describe behavior. You arrive late, spend your day reading the newspaper, take long lunch hours, and let the work pile up on your desk. You take all the good accounts for yourself and shove the unproductive ones off on subordinates. You make sure that you go to all the seminars and sales meetings held in Las Vegas, Orlando, or Honolulu.

Now you have something to work with. Are you really spending your day in unproductive pursuits? Or are you having a working breakfast before coming to the office, gaining valuable information from the *Wall Street Journal,* and using your lunch hour to cultivate clients? Is it true that you are taking all the good accounts, or do they *become* good accounts because you cultivate them with care? Do you really hog the seminars and meetings in exotic places, or have you simply enjoyed the luck of the draw?

If you conclude that the criticism is not negatively motivated, it is time to start asking questions. Your purpose is not to grill the critic as a courtroom attorney would, but to clarify the issues involved. Your questions should be aimed at turning the critic's generalities into specifics and exposing the objective facts behind the judgmental statements. If your critic says you are lazy, you will want to know what specific behavior of yours gives the impression that you are lazy. This takes the pressure off you and puts it on the critic. The critic now has to think and to produce the facts to support the accusation.

The questioning approach also shows respect for the critic. You have not gone into a childish posture of defensiveness, denial, counterattack, or withdrawal. You are showing a genuine interest in the criticism, a willingness to consider its validity and to respond positively. You will also have a better chance to gain the critic's respect. If your questions expose the lack of substance in the criticism, the critic is unlikely to approach you again unless the criticism is sound and constructive.

Once you have completed your silent observation and have explored the criticism through the questioning of your critic, you are in a position to reach an informed opinion of your own and to state it assertively. In stating your position, you do not have to put down the critic's position. It is enough that you have examined the facts objectively and have reached a conclusion based on the facts. At this point, your critic can agree or disagree with you. As a result, you have handled the criticism in a way befitting a public person.

Staying Positive in Negative Situations

Whether they are handling complaints, dealing with criticism, or confronting other obstacles to progress, public persons learn to keep positive attitudes. A positive attitude enables you to look upon problems not as barriers but as creative opportunities. Thomas Edison had a job as a telegraph operator in an era when telegraph messages were sent by audible clicks. The operator had to be able to translate these clicks into dots and dashes, which formed the letters of the Morse Code. When Edison's hearing deteriorated to the point that he could no longer hear the clicks, the young genius might have given up and sought some other occupation. Instead, he invented a telegraph that put the dots and dashes on paper, thus eliminating the need for acute hearing. It also eliminated the need for Edison to continue making a living as a telegraph operator. He was well on his way to greatness as an inventor.

Roger Fritz tells of the amateur golfer whose positive attitude under adversity enabled him to win a tournament. It was a tight contest when the golfer reached the seventeenth hole. His drive landed just short of the green, and he appeared to have an excellent chance of picking up a birdie. As he neared the ball, he realized that it had rolled into a paper bag discarded by someone in the gallery—a formidable obstacle to victory. The golfer could remove the ball from the bag at the expense of a penalty stroke. He could attempt the impossible: knock the ball out of the bag and toward the hole. Or he could come up with a creative solution. From his pocket, he drew the creative solution— a book of matches. He set fire to the paper bag, which burned away, leaving the ball exposed to his club. The golfer then chose the right club and knocked the ball into the hole.[1]

You can solve problems by following these six steps:

1. *Determine whether a problem exists.* Evaluate the situation in terms of gains and losses. If you experience a substantial gain by doing something—and suffer a substantial loss by not doing it—then you have a problem.

2. *Identify what is wrong.* Investigate the several factors that will help you determine the source of the problem. You should begin by looking at the situation beyond your immediate concern. Often we treat symptoms of problems rather than the real source; instead, we need to look beyond the microscopic view of what is happening. This probe should include personal observations of what has occurred, as well as very specific dialogues with other people who are involved with the issue. Through their eyes and yours, examine every aspect of the situation. And, if appropriate, you might want to review materials and conduct other research. In many instances it is helpful to commit what you have learned to writing so that you can review your observations with a new perspective later.

3. *Decide the facts and determine what is relevant.* Sort through your research and separate information that

is timely and important from that which is not pertinent. This exercise will help you to reinforce the significance of the information, put that information into
proper perspective, and determine which solution will
work.

4. *Create a standard of measurement.* Devise the criteria by which you will determine whether the solution
is working.

5. *Implement the solution.* Put your ideas and prob-
lem-solving techniques to work in a realistic environment and time frame.

6. *Monitor the success of the solution.* To affirm that
you have selected the appropriate solution, you will
need to regularly check its impact on the original situation. Your standards of measurement should help
you monitor the solution objectively. If you discover
that what you thought should resolve the problem is
not working, then do not hesitate to create a new
solution.

Ten Qualities of Leadership

In seeking positive public personhood, you should
strive to develop the following ten leadership attri-
butes:

1. *Public persons are active on their feet and always
on the move.* This translates into longer task-oriented
hours. Public persons persevere when others lose the
courage of their convictions. Good leaders know how
to conserve energy and store it for critical negotia-
tions. They seek out problems to solve rather then

waiting for them to strike. They assert their ideas and hold to them.

2. *Public persons constantly educate themselves.* Their storehouse of knowledge aids others who seek guidance and inspiration. Public persons read copiously and are always engaged in the learning process. They accept all the training their businesses or organizations have to offer and attend public seminars or take courses whenever possible.

3. *Public persons have good judgment.* This reflects common sense and indicates intelligence. Public persons make sure they are well-informed before they speak. They stay alert at all times and make their judgments reasonable and dependable.

4. *Public persons demonstrate positive personalities and epitomize self-confidence.* High-profile people who positively position themselves do not think about failure but instead focus only on success. Yet public persons are not afraid to make mistakes. They realize that the only way to move forward is to turn mistakes into lessons and create an atmosphere in which risk-taking is encouraged.

5. *Public persons exhibit creativity and initiative.* They can visualize new directions and translate vision into reality. Public persons maintain open minds about new possibilities for action and direction. They actively seek new ideas from their co-workers, implement worthwhile ideas, and strongly support the people who suggest them.

6. *Public persons exude enthusiasm and optimism.* They display an upbeat demeanor in front of the people they lead. These leaders find something to be positive and cheerful about each day and are sincere about it. They cultivate positive communication through

their body language, voice quality, and choice of words.

7. *Public persons inspire trust.* They possess honesty, integrity, maturity, self-respect, and respect for others. As leaders, they honor their commitments at all times.

8. *Public persons remain constant.* Consistency is important to public persons who adhere to the same standards and principles today and tomorrow. They direct the same high expectations at themselves as they direct toward others.

9. *Public persons make themselves accessible.* They pursue highly individualistic visions and adhere to the highest standards. Yet they are able to interact with people in honest, unaffected ways.

10. *Public persons give power and responsibility to others.* They enable others to learn, to make progress, to increase their influence, and to accomplish their own goals, not just those of the public person. These leaders know their greatest legacy involves finding effective people to replace them and to help those newcomers along the way.

Public persons, as we have learned, are people who are known or recognized by many people whom they themselves do not know. For this to benefit you and your organization, people must know you in positive ways. This calls for community relations. In the next chapter, I will show how community relations can enhance your image, your impact—and your income.

In Summary:

- Public persons are people who are known or recognized by many people whom they themselves do not know.

- When you are a public person, your identity lends an attention-getting quality to your name.

- A public person who wants to lead others must assume the responsibilities of leadership. The first responsibility is to know yourself, your capacities, and your limitations, including stress.

- A public person makes a powerful impact with a positive attitude and a sense of humor.

- A public person needs to learn how to deal with complaints and criticism, as well as how to remain positive in negative situations.

- A public person succeeds by demonstrating ten important criteria for leadership.

Notes

1. Roger Fritz, *You're In Charge: A Guide for Business and Personal Success* (Glenview, Ill.: Scott, Foresman, 1986), 85.

5

The Public Person and Community Relations

As I discussed in chapter 1, to succeed in business or politics you, as a public person, need to make leadership contributions to your community. This establishes a bond between you and your community and enhances your image and identity. Additionally, since you are deeply involved in projects that add real benefits to your community, people cannot help but know about you. They will form positive opinions of you and of your organization. This positive perception will strengthen your business, professional, or political prospects.

Community relations is more comprehensive than public relations. Public relations has traditionally served as a predominant "feeder" to the media. In fact, PR provides more than 70 percent of all the information that gets into print or goes out on the airwaves.

Community relations extends far beyond public relations. In community relations, *PR* stands for *Personal Return*, *Personal Reward*, and *Professional Results*. So PR has a triple application. Your personal return refers to something distinctive that you give back to your community. Your personal reward is the satisfaction you will experience from having made a contribution. Your professional results will spring from the high visibility you have created. These results can come in the form of increased business, a profitable bottom line, an enhanced public profile, and more.

Community service not only makes others feel good about you, but also makes you feel good about yourself. Further, community service can present you with creative challenges. It can offer you some of the most fulfilling aspects of your personhood and of your profession. We all need objectives. We need focus and direction. Most of all, we need the sense of accomplishment that comes from achieving what we set out to do. This is true in our personal and in our professional lives.

I learned the value of community service at an early age. When I was twelve years old, my life experiences were tearing me to pieces. My parents divorced and I went to Scottsdale, Arizona, to live for a while with my mother. Not only did I face the trauma of the divorce, but also I had to leave my family, make new friends, and, alas, find a new accordion teacher.

At that time, I had a strong feeling that I had to decide then and there what to do with my life. I narrowed it to two choices: anesthesiologist or journalist. I plunged myself into volunteer activities that would prepare me for both careers. I became a candy striper and a school newspaper writer—neither of which was a paying position. Those jobs, however, did enable me to show what I could do, and they gave me exposure. Over the next five years I accumulated nearly 1,000 hours of service to a local hospital. I also worked as a newspaper reporter and editor, a commercial radio talk-show host, and the Las Vegas High School junior-varsity football-game announcer.

These experiences focused my career thinking. I decided to become a journalist, and that led me into the world of newspapers, radio, television, and media relations—in editorial, management, and ownership capacities.

Never was the rightness of this career choice so clear as when I returned to my native Las Vegas after five years in Washington, D.C. I had been working as press secretary to Senator Harry Reid of Nevada. Coming home to Nevada provided me with vast opportunities to give something back—professionally and personally—to my family, my friends, and my community. The most satisfying contributions I made came in the form of community service, public speaking, and communication-skills education programs.

Your skills may lie in other areas. Whatever they are, they are skills your community and the people within it can use. Share them generously, and the rewards will come back to you in positive, productive ways.

Taking the Lead, Meeting the Need

Public persons do not work alone. They use their people skills to draw others to them. Their assertiveness makes public persons natural leaders. They function well in teamwork situations.

At one time or another, you have probably played "pick-up" games of softball, volleyball, or basketball. When you did, there was probably no formal procedure for choosing a leader. Usually, a leader emerged by consensus—a natural leader whom everyone was willing to follow out of respect for the leader's personality and ability. If you remember, that leader was usually the person who first said, "Hey, let's get up a team and play some ball." It works the same way in informal tasks that require group efforts. You want to become the natural leader others are willing to follow. This means you must be willing to take the initiative to propose the project.

Let's consider this principle through an example. Joe the veterinarian once boarded Rusty, a cocker spaniel belonging to Mrs. Olsen. When Mrs. Olsen came in to take Rusty home, she was accompanied by her twelve-year-old son, Denny, who was born with Down's Syndrome. When Joe saw how warmly Denny embraced his pet, his heart went out to the boy.

"He's in special classes with other mentally handicapped children," said Mrs. Olsen. "One day they had show-and-tell and Denny took Rusty to school. You should have seen the fuss the kids made over him."

After the next Rotary meeting, Joe told Victor, the president of his chapter, about the incident.

"I'll bet those kids would really get a kick out of a trip to the zoo," he said. "We should organize one for them."

"Great idea," said Victor. "Why don't you form a team and get to work on it?"

"Okay," said Joe. "Since Mrs. Olsen is a client of mine, I'll find out from her whom we should contact at the school. I often do work for the zoo, so I'm sure we can get the kids in at special prices."

Joe motioned for another member to join them. "Bill, you're the man with the car dealership. Do you think you could scrape up a demo van or two to provide transportation for some mentally challenged kids on a zoo outing?"

"You bet," said Bill. "We've got a couple of air-conditioned eleven-passenger vans on the lot right now. You tell me when, and I'll have them all cleaned and gassed up."

"Good," said Joe. "Why don't we get a half-dozen of us who are interested and let's all get together over at my house Wednesday night. We'll need drivers, chaperones, and somebody to fix picnic lunches. We can go over the details and bring the proposal back to the club at its next meeting."

Joe followed the natural process of team formation. Each person has a role, each person voluntarily fills it, and each person feels free to contribute ideas and criticism. Joe came up with the vision, and stepped naturally into the role of leader. But others showed initiative, too, and their ideas refined the vision. Together they planned the outing, had fun doing it, and were rewarded by the experience of interacting with an appealing, enthusiastic group of youngsters.

Joe's leadership did not go unrecognized. The club's publicity chairman got the word to the local newspaper, which had a photographer on hand when Joe led Denny up to the deer in the petting zoo. The caption beneath the photo identified Joe as the man who got it all started. Since then, the community has perceived Joe not only as a local veterinarian but also as a caring person with a gift for getting things accomplished.

Mrs. Olsen continues to tell all her friends about Joe's thoughtfulness. All of them who have pets now think of Joe when they need a veterinarian.

Joe has also established himself among his peers as a man of action. Those who worked on his team will keep him in mind when they have projects to carry out. They will seek him out when they go looking for team members to advance their community relations projects.

Joe exercised leadership by identifying a need that was not being filled and resolving to fill it. That is how you can become a leader. You cannot lead by going about things half-heartedly. You must have a passion for what you do. When you feel passionate about the undertaking, your passion will rub off on others. Soon they will join you.

When you see a community project that needs undertaking or a problem that needs solving, take the initiative to suggest it. Take the lead by proposing a project, and you will probably lead a team that will rally around you. You will be moving forward—toward public personhood.

Team-Building Steps

Step into your leadership role in the full confidence that you are a "creative genius." Do not undersell yourself. Go in with the conviction that whatever the task you are tackling, a successful outcome is possible.

You know that the outcome is going to benefit your community and you.

You will want to start the project by finding out why the players have signed on. People's personal agendas always affect the outcome of a project. Make sure that everyone is working toward the same objective and for the right motives. Then map out a team mission. Do this before you get together with your team. When you share your goals with the team, do not be dogmatic about it. Always show flexibility, allowing input from others.

Clearly define each person's role within the group. Power struggles occur when the roles of individual team members are vague. Create a group identity. This includes giving the group a name. People are more likely to feel that their tasks and the team goals are significant if the group sounds official.

When coaches take their teams into athletic contests, they have to draw up game plans. The same is true of teams that go into community projects. At the outset, you should indicate how people will interrelate. When the individuals know their respective roles, they are more likely to interact positively with each other and make positive contributions to the team goals.

Use the first person plural when communicating with the team, emphasizing "we" and "our" and downplaying "I" and "you." This helps team members to feel they have an ownership of the project. It is *their* project, not just yours. You also reinforce the concept of ownership when you share information with the team members. Give them the background, reasons, and priorities involved in the things they are doing.

Encourage continuity. Keep team members well

informed about dates, times, and places for team activities. Let them know what is happening next. Relaxation should also play a part in the team routine. When possible, plan your gatherings around events and places where team members can interact on a personal basis. Refreshments and sharing of food or drink creates a "family" unit and psychological bonds.

As you search for solutions and results, willingly venture in new directions. You can ignite the innate creativity in all your team members. To give this creativity free rein, you will need to develop an open atmosphere. Let your team members know that all ideas are important. Share your ideas with them and encourage them to share theirs.

Brainstorming is one of the most effective ways of eliciting creativity from a team. Remember that in brainstorming, it is necessary to suspend criticism of others. The group should consider every idea, no matter how off-the-wall it may seem. Sometimes an idea that at first seems outlandish turns out to be the creative solution you are looking for. Even wildly impractical ideas may have a germ of relevance that will trigger a more practical idea in someone else's mind. By offering unrestricted opportunity for all to contribute, you increase the number of ideas and, therefore, the likelihood that just the right idea will eventually emerge. Do not expect to come up with the ultimate idea the first time around. It may take dozens of brainstorming sessions to create a sterling result.

When I attended Las Vegas High School, my creative writing teacher taught me one of the most valuable lessons of my life. She emphasized the importance of writing something—*anything*—every day. "Be patient," she said. I realized that those brief exchanges between my brain and the writing mechanism in my hands often produced results of marginal quality at best. At some point, however, I knew that I just might create a literary masterpiece—one that would not have happened without the many days of practice that preceded it.

So brainstorm as often as necessary. Review all the possibilities. Then refine them. Make your decisions by consensus rather than by vote. Voting is divisive; one side always loses. You do not want your team split apart by winners and losers. You want all of them to think of themselves as parts of a winning team. Reinforce the team concept by praising the entire team effort, without singling out individuals.

Once you have reached consensus, turn your ideas into action. The best reward and the best reinforcement for creativity is seeing its results. This is true whether the idea works or not. You will enjoy other rewards, too. People grow to respect and admire those who want to improve their communities. The people you serve like to do business with people who make contributions to what is important to them.

Community Service Possibilities

If you analyze your own inventory of resources and talents, and put your imagination to work, you can come up with all kinds of possibilities for community service projects. Working with children and youth provides an especially fertile field for community service. Here are some possibilities:

- **Tag onto an existing program.** It could be an educational program. It could be a program aimed at preventing diseases or combatting adverse social conditions. It could be a program that provides support to victims of disease or social conditions. Find such a program and look for ways to provide assistance in the form of money, expertise, or volunteerism.

- **Develop your own program.** Example: a youth telephone "hot line" targeting children with special problems. You could promote it with posters in schools, with information in counselors' offices, or with information passed out in homerooms. Stress telephone access to help whenever the child needs it most.

- **Create "surrogate" sponsorships.** Soroptimists International of Greater Las Vegas sponsors Regina Hall, a facility for troubled teenage girls. Your organization can find worthy projects that it can adopt and give a needed boost. Civic groups have been known to become affiliated with spousal and child-abuse centers.

- **Produce literature and programs and make presentations at civic organizations.** This could involve a club-sponsored speakers bureau and one-to-one contact with troubled children.

Let me give you some examples of community relations programs I developed for three of my clients. The programs have helped these community leaders make major contributions—personal returns—to their communities while enabling them to reap personal rewards and professional bottom-line results.

The Training Station is a statewide computer training facility that teaches one- and two-day classes in dozens of computer programs. One spring, owner Dawn Buffery strengthened her business by adding community relations to her plan. She volunteered her facilities and skills to her local school district to teach modified survey courses to academically talented elementary students.

"We have a responsibility to use our own skills to help our children—our community's children—to learn and progress," she said.

Lynn Maguire Physical Therapy is a full-range rehabilitation facility. Maguire also provides a two-part "back school" to teach patients critical essentials for back care and injury prevention. Maguire decided to contribute her own "personal return" to the community. She is a major sponsor of the Arthritis Foundation Telethon, which raises money to aid in arthritis research and in treatment of its victims. She also offers the foundation the use of her pool facilities and aquatics therapy.

The World Volleyball Championships for the Disabled were held in the United States for the first time in Las Vegas in July 1989. These championships provided demonstration, participation, and inspiration to people in our community, state, nation, and world. The participants left Las Vegas and our nation with a positive international image. Beyond that, they provided physically challenged people with the psychological and physical resources to participate and to challenge themselves and others. Dan Mushett, who directed the event, gave hundreds of passes to disabled residents of southern Nevada and to civic groups and volunteers. In return, the event attracted daily news coverage in local and regional newspapers and on television and radio. The championships also received exposure on national wire services and in several city-wide newsletters. The event thus obtained free publicity that otherwise would have cost its backers many thousands of dollars.

In each of the cases I have described, personal return *to* the community resulted in bottom-line professional results *from* the community. The cases mentioned here involve three very different avenues of helping the community. They were based on the skills and resources of the individuals who did the giving. In each case, my approach was to customize programs to the individual, with the objective of turning public relations into community relations. You too can find ways to benefit your community, as an individual or as an organization. Find a need and resolve to fill it. Form a team and take the lead. You will be building the kind of record to make you a positive, contributing public person. Then, as this public person, you will be ready for the next step—getting your message out to other people. The next chapter will tell how to do that.

In Summary:

- To experience effective public personhood, you should get involved in your community. Through community relations, you cause people to form positive opinions of you, and their esteem produces healthier prospects for your business or organization.

- Community relations goes beyond public relations. It involves your giving something distinctive and substantive to the community. Those who give of themselves also receive—in the form of community recognition and esteem—which also can produce a healthy impact on the bottom line of your business.

- Public persons demonstrate leadership. This means identifying a community need, resolving to fill it, and forming a team to accomplish the task.

- You can become involved in a community project by tagging onto an existing program, developing your own program, creating surrogate sponsorships, or producing literature and programs on a subject vital to the public welfare.

- You should base involvement on your own interests, skills, and resources.

6

Gaining Access to the Media

Everyone who has lived on a farm knows what a hen does after she has laid an egg. She cackles. In that way, the whole barnyard knows about her accomplishment, and so does the farmer. A productive hen is a valuable asset to the farm. She will get a snug nest and choice food. And when it comes time for Sunday dinner, she will not end up in the pot.

In the business and social worlds, laying an egg has quite a different connotation, but we still can learn from the barnyard hen. When you have accomplished something positive, it is good to herald the news. You could do this by cackling—spreading the tidings by word of mouth to as many people as you can reach. But it is far more efficient to do it via the mass media. The public person learns to master the art of using the media.

Publicity and Advertising

The media offer two main avenues for carrying your message to the public: publicity and advertising. The most obvious difference between the two is that publicity is free while advertising costs. The cost of your advertising message will depend on its length, the medium you select to deliver your message, and the number of people the medium reaches.

Through advertising, as opposed to publicity, you can exercise some control over the message. You can specify the wording, the length, and sometimes even the position. You can repeat the message as often as you are willing to pay for it.

With publicity, you sacrifice control but gain credibility. People tend to put more confidence in what the publication or electronic medium says about you than in what you say about yourself through a paid advertisement. First, however, you will need to persuade the media to say positive things about you. We will go into more detail about how to do that later in this chapter. For now, let's look at the basic requirements for access to the news media.

What Is News?

A news organization will evaluate your publicity message on the basis of newsworthiness. If you ask an editor to define newsworthiness, you may get an answer reminiscent of the comment of Potter Stewart, associate justice of the Supreme Court, when he sought a legal definition of pornography: "I can't define it, but I know what it is when I see it."

Editors like to refer to a thing called "news sense"—an instinct for what the public wants to know. While much about news judgment is subjective, editors and newscasters do look for some identifiable characteristics in a story.

First, the story has to be *timely*. The more recent an event, the more newsworthy. If it has an identifiable bearing on great events currently in the headlines, its newsworthiness is enhanced. For example, your trip to Moscow in 1991 might not have created a flurry of interest under ordinary circumstances. But if you happened to be in Red Square at the time of the abortive Kremlin coup, your comments might have generated a keen interest on the part of your hometown newspaper.

News organizations also look for a story that is *distinctive*. Recall the example in chapter 1 of my client who gained local and eventually national publicity because he shipped his products in an unusual kind of packing material—popcorn. If something is not distinctive in some way, it is less likely to be considered newsworthy. Nobody reports on the number of airplanes that take off and land safely every day of the year. It is news, however, when an airplane does *not* take off and land safely. Nobody writes a story about the bank teller who serves loyally, faithfully, and honestly day in and day out. Bank tellers are expected to do that. It is the embezzler who gets the headlines, because embezzling is out of the norm. Realize that the media are not necessarily cynical; however, their people are trained to look for unusual reporting angles. Since things go reasonably well most of the time, it is the few times when they do *not* go well that tend to get the attention.

Contrary to myth, media people are not averse to printing good news. They are always on the lookout for the helpful, the heartwarming, the humorous, the inspiring, and the bizarre. If your message fits any of those descriptions, it stands a better chance of making the headlines or the newscasts.

In addition to being distinctive, an event must *stimulate interest for a significant number of people.* The more people the story interests, the more newsworthy it is. That interest may be direct and affect a large number of people personally or it can have a secondary or emotional impact on those people. For example, the trauma of a child with a life-threatening disease who needs an organ transplant directly affects that child and the immediate family. However, when the community takes an interest in the child's welfare, that entire community is emotionally affected by this story.

Obviously, the significance of a news event depends upon the universe served by the news medium. A barbecue in support of the volunteer rescue squad may make the headlines in a town of 4,000 people, but it will get little or no ink in the *Los Angeles Times.* A new fast-food restaurant may be big news in a small town, but it will not make the *Wall Street Journal.*

Do not let this reality dismay you. If you are striving to become a public person in your hometown, you do not have to aim for the giant media. It is easier to gain access to those media that serve small universes—the universes in which most of us live.

In many large metropolitan areas, the big-city dailies often subdivide their large universes into several smaller universes through neighborhood zoned editions. These zoned editions—often tabloids within the broadsheet main newspaper—cover neighborhoods the way small-town newspapers cover their communities. If you are turned away by the business, features, or lifestyles section, ask whether the newspaper has a zoned edition serving your area.

If you have decided to take out an advertisement, the small local newspaper or the local zoned edition of a metropolitan daily may be your most cost-effective medium. It does not make sense to pay $1,000 to have your message delivered to 500,000 subscribers if only 5,000 of those subscribers are potential clients or customers. The local newspaper or zoned edition will reach fewer people, but they may be precisely the people you want to reach—your *target audience*—and you will not be paying for the privilege of reaching all those people who will never do business with you.

Even if you are seeking free visibility, do not overlook the advantages of targeting your audience. If you have a national clientele, a column inch in the *Wall Street Journal* may be more valuable than ten inches in your small-town daily. If your clientele come from an area within commuting distance of your office, you may be better served by the local paper. And it is much easier to get the attention of the local editor.

Media Options

The newspaper, of course, is just one of several media available to the public person. The print media also include general-population and specialty magazines, trade and business publications, and newsletters of various sorts. All of these can be international, national, regional, or local in scope.

The electronic media have become the dominant sources of news for hundreds of millions of people around the world. Traditionally, people have looked to the television newscast for daily summaries of the news. They have turned on the radio for hourly updates throughout the day. In the 1980s the world gained an even faster access to news events. Cable News Network (CNN) revolutionized electronic journalism by reporting events in progress to a worldwide audience. In addition, CNN stimulated an awareness in even the smallest communities of how cablecasting can impact news and information dissemination at the community level.

Each medium has its advantages and drawbacks. While newspapers and other publications can expand their "news holes" to fit the demands of the day, the electronic medium's "news hole" is finite. Newspapers can print more pages, but radio and television stations cannot produce more hours in the day. Also, most electronic media—radio and television (both broadcast and cablecast)—primarily provide entertainment and devote a relatively small portion of their time to news and public service announcements. Hence, the electronic media in most communities must shepherd their time and be much more selective in the material they use. You will find expanded opportunities in larger cities that have all-news radio stations, television stations with longer and more frequent newscasts and public service programs, and cable companies that dedicate channels for news and public affairs programming.

Any medium's effectiveness depends on which and how many people it reaches. Newspapers and magazines rely on the publications' circulation. In the United States and Canada, radio and television ownership is practically universal, but not everyone subscribes to newspapers or magazines. In many regions, the market may be divided among several newspapers, while each radio and television signal can reach an entire region.

Radio, broadcast, and cablecast stations have the advantage of providing news and information spontaneously to the public; however, this spontaneity can also be a disadvantage because electronic news is a perishable commodity. If the listeners or viewers are not tuned in at the time your message is delivered, they have lost it—unless they had the foresight to record it in some way. Your published message, though, is permanently inscribed in paper and ink, and is available for reading and re-reading as long as you keep the newspaper, magazine, or other publication. In addition, published materials can be easily clipped, shared with others, pasted in scrapbooks, or filed for posterity on microfilm or compact discs.

Newspapers are designed to reach a general audience; therefore, if you are targeting a more specific audience, the newspaper may not be your most effective medium. You may look for a specialty publication that reaches the specific audience you are targeting— perhaps a professional journal, a sports magazine, a hobby-oriented newsletter, or a youth-focused entertainment periodical.

Or you may want to convey your message electronically to distinct audiences by focusing on special programs or delivering your information at particular times of the day or days of the week. Radio stations, though they beam their signals toward every set within range, are able to target certain audiences by developing formats and programs that appeal to the people they want to reach. The radio station's audience will depend upon whether its principal fare is easy listening, hard rock, soft rock, jazz, country and western, talk, or news. Choose your station according to the audience you want to reach.

Television, of course, offers the advantages of sight, sound, and immediacy. A few moments in front of television cameras can give you a powerful opportunity to project a positive image to the public. Television reaches a large audience, and the majority of people today get most of their information from the tube. However, you do not have to aim solely for the six o'clock and eleven o'clock newscasts. Many radio, broadcast, and cablecast stations also have local talk shows that offer the public person opportunities for exposure. Their producers are always looking for someone with an interesting story to tell or some useful expertise to share. Find out about these shows and get acquainted with the producers. In addition, stations run public service announcements and community billboards, at no charge, to help you deliver your nonprofit messages.

Compartments of the Media

When you call a newspaper and ask to speak to the editor, the person who answers the telephone will probably say, "Which one?" Even a moderate-sized daily may have many editors. In the early days of journalism, "the editor" was often the owner, and was considered the personification of the newspaper. Today, when you write a "letter to the editor," you are not writing to a specific individual, but to the newspaper itself.

Here is a quick look at who has the final word at most newspapers: the publisher is usually the chief operating officer, if not the CEO, of the newspaper. The publisher is the person who has purview over each of the operational functions of the newspaper: news/editorial, advertising, production, and circulation.

The content of newspapers and many other types of for-profit publications is provided by news/editorial and advertising. These two departments have a church-and-state type of separation and are protective of their roles and their space in each issue. Most news departments resent it when advertising people come to them with stories about businesses that advertise in the publication. They regard these requests as attempts to compromise the integrity of the news report. News departments fiercely contend that the amount of business an advertiser does with the publication has no bearing on how that advertiser is treated in the news. This separation issue, however, is not exclusive to print journalism; radio and television news directors are equally concerned about the integrity of their news operations. Though decision makers involved in both print and electronic journalism strive for this detachment, many might question whether or not it is a reality.

If you want to have your message published or electronically transmitted and you know the advertising representative, ask that account executive for the name of the news person to contact. Do not ask the account executive to make the contact for you. That request could doom your accessibility to the person who can help you get your message to the public.

Categories of Advertising

The three broad categories of advertising are retail, classified, and national. Classified ads are used by businesses and individuals to advertise specific products or services. Examples of this type of advertising include help wanted, positions wanted, real estate, automobile sales, and other "for sale" categories.

Retail ads usually advertise the business or organization rather than specific products. Local or regional merchants ordinarily place them, and they usually produce the bulk of a newspaper's revenue.

National advertising refers to advertising on a national scale by companies that place the same or similar ads in media across the country. Westinghouse, for instance, might use national advertising to promote its refrigerators in the top 100 retail markets. Family Home Appliances on Main Street in Yourtown would use retail advertising to promote its entire business, including, perhaps, Westinghouse refrigerators.

News and Editorial

News and editorial mark another church-state type of boundary on the media. The news department, in theory, is concerned with reporting the straight facts, regardless of the individual biases of reporters and editors. The editorial department or editorial director provides the opinion content, usually through an editorial page, an opposite-editorial page (often called op-ed or op-edit), a Sunday commentary section, or editorial commentary at the end of a newscast.

In newspaper and other publications, the top news executive often wears the title of executive editor. This person usually holds sway over sports, features, business, and other special departments, as well as the local, state, national, and international news functions. In radio and television operations, the top news executive is usually the news director, whose functions parallel those of the newspaper executive editor. However, because most electronic news operations have smaller staffs than newspapers, every person in the newsroom, including the news director, can be called upon to perform multiple tasks, such as reporting, videotaping, editing, producing, and more.

A newspaper's editorial page editor presides over a smaller domain—a staff of editors and writers who produce the newspaper's own editorials and who are responsible for the op-edit pages and commentary sections. Sometimes the editorial page is a one-person show. Most medium-sized newspapers have from two to four editorial writers. Larger newspapers may have a dozen or more. In radio and television, editorials are often written by top management or the owners. In larger cities, radio and television stations often have editorial directors on staff to craft commentaries that define their stations' positions on issues.

The managing editor is the overall newsroom supervisor, usually having charge of local, state, and national news. On smaller newspapers, the features, sports, and business editors may also report to the managing editor, and he becomes, in effect, the executive editor. Most radio and television stations also have managing editors who perform similar functions.

Newspapers, unlike most radio and television stations, often have city editors to oversee the local reporters and directly supervise day-to-day local coverage. The number of other editors will depend upon the size of the newspaper. Sometimes an editor will wear several hats. The business editor may also be the real estate editor, the automotive editor, and the travel editor. The features editor may also be the fashion editor and the entertainment editor.

Editor & Publisher Yearbook, which is available at most libraries, is an annual directory of the newspaper industry. It contains a list of executives and editors of daily and weekly newspapers, together with information on addresses, telephone numbers, circulation, and ownership. *Broadcasting Yearbook* provides similar information as it applies to the radio and television industry.

On the front line of every news medium are the reporters who actually gather the information that goes into news and feature stories. As a public person, you will find it helpful to become acquainted with the local reporters who cover your field of interest. If you live in a small town, get to know the reporters and editors from your local paper and the reporters from the local bureau of the metropolitan newspaper serving your area. You can also expand your visibility by contacting reporters at major national and international professional and trade publications when you have credible and timely information to share with them.

As I explained, the electronic media usually have smaller and less specialized news staffs than newspapers do. Therefore, in addition to familiarizing yourself with the news directors, you will need to know the program directors and public affairs directors. If you want to have more control over how your message is prepared and transmitted, you can work with their sales staffs to buy commercial time or program blocs. However, you can gain positive visibility, without spending substantial sums of money, by participating in special events and community projects sponsored by radio and television stations.

For example, KVBC-TV, the NBC affiliate in Las Vegas, interacts very strongly with the community. One annual event, Earth Fair, involves the entire community and gives people and organizations the opportunity to participate publicly in the all-day event. Organizations can co-sponsor the event, enter booths, provide transportation for visitors, and more.

An easier pathway for most people to access radio and television audiences to promote events is through public service announcements and community calendars. Generally, stations run these only for nonprofit events. So this is a great way for you to volunteer your expertise and get public recognition for it.

Become the Expert

You can obtain valuable exposure through print and electronic media by establishing yourself as an "expert" in your field. News people often need to call on the experts for comment when developments occur in a particular field. Let's say your field is real estate. When the interest rates change, news desks are often eager to know how this will affect the real-estate market. Whom do they call? They call the people who they know are thoroughly familiar with real estate and who are articulate in talking about it. If you meet those criteria, the media may not only seek you out frequently, but they may also quote you by name and title. They may even include a picture of you to accompany the story.

This kind of exposure works as free advertising. When an individual decides to buy or sell a house, whose name will pop into mind? The person seen or heard or read about as an authority on real estate.

Vehicles for Conveying Your Message

Now that you, the expert, know where to go and who to see to get your message before the public, let's consider the vehicle for carrying your message to the media.

The most familiar vehicle for conveying your message is the news release. The news release is valuable to the news media because it saves them the trouble and expense of interviewing you, organizing the material, and writing it. If your news release is well prepared, the newspaper or station may run it with few, if any, changes. Later, we will discuss the details of news release writing.

For major announcements, you might want to prepare a media packet. This might include a news release, one or more photographs, a brochure on your organization and, when appropriate, background statistics. If you do not have a brochure, a background sheet with basic information on you and your organization will work.

News releases may provide radio and television stations with information they can use as news items or public service announcements. Remember that the electronic media can seldom deal with the length and detail of a newspaper story, and the six o'clock news can only devote time to the top news of the day.

Radio and television do, however, offer other vehicles for spreading your message. As I mentioned earlier, the advertising commercial or "spot" gives you an opportunity to write your own script and have it broadcast—for a fee.

When you are representing a nonprofit, tax-exempt organization, the public service announcement offers you a free publicity vehicle. In the United States, the Federal Communications Commission, which licenses radio and television stations and assigns their frequencies, expects stations to devote a certain amount of air time to public service. Therefore, stations are willing to give free time to announcements involving community activities by social, educational, religious, charitable, civic, or service organizations.

Ordinarily, announcers will read public service announcements over the air several times a day, usually in clusters with other PSAs. Some radio stations, however, accept pretaped PSAs. Your message will probably be condensed to ten to thirty seconds. A ten-second announcement allows about thirty to forty words. You can get 80 to 100 words into a thirty-second announcement and 160 to 200 words into a sixty-second announcement. Obviously, brevity is the key to successful PSA writing.

Some stations ask you to submit a standard one-page news release that answers the five W's: *Who, What, When, Where,* and *Why*. In addition to supplying this information, do not forget to include, at the top, the name of the sponsoring organization and the names and phone numbers of contacts. Other stations ask for a news release and a script; still others want only a script.

Your public service announcement should get straight to the point. You do not have time for flowery introductions. Keep your sentences short and simple and use familiar words that are easy to pronounce. When you have finished writing, read your copy aloud. If you find trouble enunciating certain words, look for easily pronounced synonyms. If you find even mild tongue-twisters in the copy, rephrase. Listen to the public service announcements over the stations you are trying to reach. Note their formats and the way they are worded. Try to make your announcement sound like one of theirs.

Most newspapers have community billboard columns and events calendars that briefly inform the public of coming events or of personal and business accomplishments. Many radio and television stations have similar slots. Familiarize yourself with the contents and formats of the media outlets you want to use, and be alert for opportunities to insert positive messages about yourself. The essential information in such announcements should consist of the name of your organization; a description of the activity, date, place, and time; the reason for the event; and information on cost and how to obtain tickets. At the top of the PSA you will also want to list primary and secondary contact names, their telephone numbers, and the hours the station can call them for further information.

Both print and electronic outlets offer you opportunities to respond to news stories. Newspapers have editorial pages and op-edit pages; radio and television stations often schedule editorial responses. The letters-to-the-editor column is one of the most widely read features in the newspaper. Editors welcome brief, pointed, well-written letters expressing personal viewpoints; radio and television executives often allow guest commentaries or editorial responses for the same reason.

Look for opportunities to make positive observations through the letters section and editorial responses. Observe them to see what issues are on the minds of the people in your community. When you see an opportunity to use your expertise to shed a positive light on a public issue, write a letter to the editor or ask for the opportunity to do a guest column or commentary.

When you or your company has done something to merit an accolade, take advantage of the letters-to-the-editor section. You may not want to write a letter commending yourself; that could give people a negative impression of you. You can, however, ask friends to write letters under their own names lauding the good deeds you have done. You might even write a few letters yourself and hand them out to friends to sign and send to the editor.

Most newspapers limit the length of letters and many limit the frequency with which they will print letters from an individual. Even when formal limits on length do not exist, however, the shorter, punchier letters are the ones that editors are most likely to publish. A typical limit on length is 200 words. Some newspapers limit writers to no more than one letter in a single thirty, sixty, or ninety day period. Most newspapers require that letters be signed, and some require addresses and telephone numbers for verification purposes. Similarly, radio and television stations impose certain restrictions; they are particularly concerned about the length of the message.

On occasions when you believe you can bring special expertise or perspective to a public issue, try submitting a guest column to the editorial page editor of your local newspaper or professional journal. These columns can run much longer than letters to the editor, and they can provide excellent showcases for your expertise. Editors often will identify you not only through your byline but also through a note at the end of the article explaining who you are and the basis of your expertise.

Once publication editors and reporters know that you are available and that you possess useful expertise, they may call on you as a story resource. When news developments arise on which you can shed light, reporters may call you for comments and quote you in their news articles. Such visibility reinforces your public personhood.

When you have reached this level of public recognition, it is helpful to anticipate the occasions when reporters or editors will call you and put you on the spot. Give careful thought to how you will respond and what you will say. Have prepared statements that you can read or hand to the reporters or broadcasters. This will safeguard you against slips of the tongue and lessen the likelihood that you will be misquoted.

You do not have to wait for the media to call you to get this kind of exposure, though. When an event transpires, and you have some expertise on the subject, call the appropriate editor or news director and say, "This is Jerry Devoe at Triple A International Financial Services. With the tax deadline seven days away, I thought your readers (or listeners or viewers) might be interested in some tips on how to prepare their tax returns in a timely, accurate way. . . ."

While news releases make up a major portion of media news content, newspapers and television and radio stations, as a matter of pride, like to showcase their own staff-produced work. A staff-written story about you, your organization, or your project will probably get better play than a news release written by an outside source and processed by the newspaper.

So to enhance your chances for coverage, you can call the appropriate reporter or editor and suggest a good feature that will highlight you or your organization. And remember, be prepared with a good reason for them to cover your story, based on its timeliness, distinctiveness, and universality.

Take Advantage of Newsletters

Organizational newsletters offer another means of conveying your message. Many organizations, from civic clubs to chambers of commerce, send out newsletters to their memberships. If you provide them with helpful tips or information tailored to the organizational membership, they will frequently publish it and credit it to you. Though newsletters rarely reach as many people as the news media, they will probably reach just the people you want to influence.

And you do not need to rely on other organizations to get your message out. You can produce your own newsletter. Once you identify the people you want to reach, send them a regular mailer full of helpful suggestions drawn from your expertise. With today's word-processors and desktop publishing equipment, these newsletters can be produced quickly and inexpensively.

If your field is real estate, for instance, you might identify a particular subdivision that is experiencing healthy sales. Send a regular newsletter to the people in that subdivision, giving them tips on buying and selling their homes and letting them know why this is a good time to buy or sell. The newsletter might not draw immediate response. However, it puts your name and the name of your business in front of the people you want to reach. When they do decide to put their homes on the market, whose name do you think they will remember?

Preparing the News Release

Chances are that your most frequently used entree to the news media will be the news release. Before you begin preparing one, keep in mind what specifics the media expect from a news source. Providing this interest-riveting information will increase the chances that your message will reach the eyes and ears of the public.

Two of the most important considerations that confront an editor are deadlines and information overload. You want to remember that editors are inundated with news releases every day and many of these are either too late or totally unacceptable. For example, do not submit a news release to an editor or news director an hour before deadline—and expect it to be used—when that release should have been submitted three days earlier. Also, avoid delivering a news release that is sloppy, incomplete, handwritten, poorly typed, filled with typographical errors, or otherwise ill-prepared. You can be assured that this release will receive, at best, a cursory look; it will probably be tossed into the garbage before the editor reads the first sentence.

In addition to serious consideration of deadlines and adequate preparation, you will want to answer the following questions to increase the probability of use for your news release:

- **Is it honest?** If a reporter or editor finds that you are deliberately submitting false or misleading information, your credibility is dead, and this and any future news releases you might submit are doomed. The media are in business to provide honest information. If they consistently give false or incomplete information, they soon lose their readers or listeners. When the media use your release, they rely on you to be honest with them so that they can be honest with their audiences.

- **Are you maintaining your integrity?** You want to honor your word in every interaction with the media. Remember that you do not always get a second chance at building a relationship with the media. It is equally important that you recognize that your reputation can open or close doors.

- **Is it accurate?** Be sure of your facts, even the trivial ones. Double-check names, titles, dates, and locations. Because editors do not have time to check all your facts behind you, they rely on you to provide accurate information. If the information proves to be inaccurate, editors will remember it and your next news release could go straight into the wastebasket.

- **Is it newsworthy?** Of course, to you, the news release meets all of the criteria any editor could possibly have. However, you must pay special attention to this consideration. Sometimes you can enhance the news value of an event by using a little initiative and a little imagination. Your barbecue to benefit the rescue squad might be of marginal interest ordinarily. Suppose, however, the governor plans to attend the event; this additional fact considerably increases the news value. What if you arrange to hold the barbecue during Fire Prevention Week in a field where there is an old barn or abandoned dwelling? In addition, the firefighters and the governor plan to set fire to the building, then put it out to demonstrate the effectiveness of their equipment and their firefighting techniques. Now your news release can take on the power of novelty.

- **Is it in the right format?** Study the medium you are trying to penetrate. If it is a publication that consists of short, punchy articles, keep your release short. If you are submitting an item for a column of news briefs that devotes one paragraph to each item, do not submit several paragraphs, and do not "cheat" by writing one full-page paragraph. If you are aiming toward a radio or television station, become familiar with the requirements for brevity. If the station specifies that a public service announcement must be just thirty-two characters long, do not send a two-page release.

    If you are dealing with a publication, notice its style for punctuation, abbreviations, and the use of numbers and symbols. Does it spell out "percent," or does it use the % symbol? Does it use honorary and courtesy titles on second reference? Associated Press style calls for spelling out single-digit numbers, to use figures for numbers from ten through 999,999, and to use a combination of words and figures for numbers from one million up. If you are planning to do a lot of news releases, you may be able to obtain an AP Stylebook through your newspaper.

- **Is it going to the right person and place?** You will benefit substantially by being familiar with the media outlets you are dealing with and the departments that will handle your information. This will help you decide more intelligently whether to direct your release to the business editor, the features or lifestyles editor, the city editor, or some other editor's desk. Getting your release to the right person greatly enhances its chances of being published. You will also score points if you address your release to the individual by name, with the proper spelling and correct job title. Learn who the various editors and reporters are, and keep abreast of any personnel changes. You will get better results when you double-check this information before you distribute your news release.

• **Is your name and telephone number on the release?** Nobody's perfect, and few of us can predict all the questions an editor or reporter might have about a release. So news people always appreciate a name and telephone number to enable them to verify information in the release, to double-check the spellings of proper names, or to clarify any questions they might have. It also benefits the reporter to have a second person's name and number if you are not available. If possible, make yourself available beyond normal working hours because many journalists are assigned to the night shift and might need timely access to you for more information. This can mean the difference between the use or non-use of your story.

Writing the Release

Now we come to the writing of a release. Many people feel intimidated by the writing of news stories. A few simple rules will help you write releases that should sail past editors with minimal editing.

The media still prefer the inverted pyramid arrangement for routine news stories. The inverted pyramid is an ancient newspaper principle and it means simply this: lead with your most important information and tell the rest in descending order of significance. That is why journalists refer to the first paragraph as "the lead." The lead should be a short, simple statement of what the story is about. Remember, as I mentioned earlier in this chapter, you need to answer the questions "Who?" "What?" "When?" "Where?" and "Why?" Here is a typical news lead:

> **The Maison du Boeuf Restaurant will cater a barbecue outing starting at noon Saturday at Riverside Park. Manager Robert Viand said the proceeds will benefit the Twin Forks Volunteer Rescue Squad.**

The lead has all the elements: *Who?* The Maison du Boeuf Restaurant, through its manager, Robert Viand. *What?* A barbecue outing. *When?* Starting at noon Saturday. *Where?* At Riverside Park. *Why?* To raise money for the rescue squad.

Once you have written your lead, the rest of the story will fall into place. You can use the remaining paragraphs to explain *how, what's next, so what,* and other details.

Remember to keep your sentences short and simple. You should limit yourself to one idea per sentence. This will prevent your sentences from rambling and make them easier to follow and comprehend.

Tell your story in the active voice. That means to let your subjects *do* things rather than having things done to them. "The train hit the cow" is a much stronger sentence than "The cow was hit by the train." Let your workhorse sentence consist of a subject followed closely by a verb followed closely by an object. Notice how a surplus of phrases and clauses clutters this sentence:

> While negotiating a blind curve on a downgrade near Sullivan's Crossing, a diesel-powered Santa Fe railroad locomotive, which was pulling a string of 100 freight cars loaded with produce from California farms and orchards at a high rate of speed, struck a prize Hereford steer belonging to the Lazy K Ranch in Cactus County.

Note how much more effectively the sentence tells the story when the clutter is removed and the simple subject/verb/object formula is followed:

> A fast Santa Fe freight train struck a prize steer on a blind curve near Sullivan's Crossing early Monday.

You can easily identify the subject, verb, and object: A *train* (subject) *struck* (verb) a *steer* (object). This simple sentence capsulizes the story and sets the stage for successive sentences to tell what the freight was hauling, who owned the steer, and probably more important, what happened to the train and the steer after the crash.

With radio and television, brevity is mandatory. Therefore, it pays to know how to pack a maximum of information into a minimum of words. Learn to substitute one-word modifiers for clauses and prepositional phrases. In the sentence above, notice how the single word "fast" took the place of six words—"at a high rate of speed."

Your sentences also become stronger when you substitute descriptive verbs for adjectives and adverbs. Do not write, "The man walked through the snow with slow and heavy steps," when you can write, "The man trudged through the snow."

Write news releases for the electronic media in a "spoken" style—using the words and syntax people normally use in everyday speech.

When you are writing a release, recognize the difference between a news story and an advertisement. In an advertisement, you are free to express your opinion and extol your business to your heart's content. You are paying for the space or the time, and within reasonable bounds of propriety, the newspaper or station will let you say what you want to say. In a news story, however, you must confine yourself to *objective* information. It is the newspaper's space, or the station's time, and they make a careful distinction between news and opinion.

So do not try to sneak free advertising messages into your release. Do not write, "Olympic Sporting Goods, which has provided quality goods for discriminating sportsmen for more than thirty years, is sponsoring a 'Hike for the Homeless' next Friday, according to Jim Morris, the friendly and engaging proprietor of the city's leading sporting goods store." If you write that, the crackling sound you'll hear will come from your release, being wadded up and hurled into a metal receptacle.

Sometimes you can insert your personal opinion into the release through a direct quotation. Even then, the opinion should not be blatantly self-serving. Editors are very leery of including material that might be interpreted as free advertising, and for very good reason. The business community reads the newspaper and listens to the broadcasts, and if the newspaper or station offers free advertising to one business, all the others will demand equal treatment.

How might the Olympic Sporting Goods release be worded? Try this:

> Olympic Sporting Goods of Ourtown will sponsor a Hike for the Homeless from City Hall to Waterworks Road starting Saturday at 10 A.M.
>
> Jim Morris, owner of Olympic, said the store will offer free refreshments for participants at the end of the hike. It will present "Hike for the Homeless" T-shirts to all participants and will award a new pair of Nike running shoes to the hiker raising the most money for the Ourtown Homeless Shelter.
>
> "We believe that if the social problems plaguing our nation are to be solved in our lifetime, business must take the lead," said Morris. "This is our way of promoting fitness among the general population and compassion for the less fortunate among us. I plan to be among the hikers, and Olympic will sponsor a number of participants. This is our way of literally walking our talk."

Notice that nowhere in this article does the writer attempt an overt "sales pitch" for the sporting goods store. Instead, the release objectively relates the story of what Olympic is doing and lets the owner tell, in his own words, why he is doing it. The sales pitch is not necessary. People who read the story will remember that Olympic was involved in a community project that promoted fitness and compassion. When consumers are ready to buy sporting goods, they will remember Olympic favorably and will think of its owner as one of the town's benevolent and responsible public persons.

By Mail, Fax, or in Person?

It is all right to mail or to hand-deliver news releases to the media. If you are blanketing the media, you may find it impractical to hand-deliver the releases. Be sure, though, that you are mailing or faxing the release to the right person. With faxes it is also beneficial to call ahead to let the recipient know when to expect the faxed release.

If you are dealing with only one or two media, you might benefit from dropping by and introducing yourself to the appropriate editor or news director. If you choose to do this, find out in advance the convenient time. If you call on an editor a few minutes before deadline, you are likely to get little more than snarls and glares. Call at the editor's convenience and be considerate of the editor's time. Remember, on a daily newspaper or an evening broadcast, an editor or news director may not be able to push things aside until the next hour or the next day. What gets into tomorrow's paper or on tonight's six o'clock news must be written, edited, and otherwise processed in time for the impending deadline.

Once you have submitted a news release, it is in the hands of the people at the publication or the station. Do not bother to call to ask whether they received the release and whether they plan to publish it or broadcast it. Even in moderately sized communities, editors and news directors can receive more than 100 news releases every day, and they are not likely to keep a log of the ones they have passed along for rewrite. And you certainly do not gain favor when you pressure them to run your story.

Editors and news directors may seem cantankerous, arbitrary, and capricious at times, but beneath their cynical facades, they are also human. They will vigorously disavow any hint of bias, but the rule applies to them as much as to anyone else: be cordial to these decision makers and let them know that you respect their craft and are willing to play by their rules. They will probably reward your attitude by going out of their way to accommodate you.

Your releases may not be published exactly the way you want, but in the long run the media exposure will be valuable to you. You will gain favorable recognition in your community. You will attain an identity for your contributions to community welfare. And you will secure public personhood, with all the benefits and responsibilities that status conveys.

In Summary:

- Public persons can position themselves effectively by mastering the art of using the media.

- The two avenues of media communications are publicity and advertising. Advertising costs, but gives you control over the message. Publicity is free, but requires you to play by the media's rules.

- For your story to be newsworthy, it must be timely, distinctive, and affect a significant number of people.

- The most effective medium for your message is the one that most successfully reaches the people you want to reach, e.g., your potential customers or clients.

- Public persons need to learn how the media are organized so that they can direct their high-visibility efforts toward the proper department and the proper individual.

- Among the vehicles for publicity are:

  1. News and feature releases.
  2. Media packets.
  3. Prepared statements and reactions.
  4. Public service announcements.
  5. Letters to the editor and editorial responses.
  6. Guest columns and commentaries.
  7. Newsletters.
  8. Events columns and community billboards.

- News releases should be honest, accurate, neat, and legible. You should submit them well ahead of the deadline for publication or broadcast, and should address them to the proper person and department. They should contain the name and telephone number of a person the editor can contact for additional information.

• You should write your news releases simply and objectively, in the inverted-pyramid style.

7

When the Media Come to You

There comes the time in your status as a public person when you are no longer just a suitor. Once the media realize who you are and where your expertise and interests lie, they will come to you. Once you become involved in, and identified with, activities that attract public attention, the media will seek you out. Sometimes they will come to you when you would rather they didn't. By achieving media mastery, however, you can learn to reap positive benefits from each experience.

When reporters call you, you are no longer trying to interest the media in a story that you want published or broadcast. You are the quarry now. They want to draw from you information to fill out the stories *they* want to develop.

This presents you with a challenge and an opportunity. They are going to write a story about you or your organization; you will not be writing it, and you will not be controlling its content. It could reflect favorably or unfavorably on you. Your responses to the reporter's questions, and the relationship you establish with the reporter, can determine whether you are going to come out looking like a champ or like a chump.

If you or your organization has been caught in a brushfire of controversy, it is particularly important that you deal with the media in a skillful, professional manner. Although you may not be able to put out the fire completely, you may keep the reporter from spreading the flames.

The key to successful media relations is found in fifteen standard rules for interaction with the media. They are:

1. *When a reporter or other media person calls, take the call.* Not only is this a standard professional courtesy, but it is also an opportunity to help you get your message to the media.

2. *Return the call immediately or as soon as possible on the day the call comes in.* Most reporters have daily or hourly deadlines, and are often competing with other media. They are not likely to delay their stories a full day just to get your comment. It is more likely that reporters will prepare their stories without your remarks. If they do, the spot that could have accommodated your version of the story might be occupied by a report that goes something like this: "Alice Jones could not be reached for comment" or "Joe Miller did not return a reporter's call." These statements can create damaging innuendo.

3. *Be thorough.* Do not omit relevant details, even if

certain information is not sought. If the reporter senses that you are not leveling or that you are deliberately withholding information, your chances of sympathetic treatment go out the window. If it appears that the reporter is poorly informed or does not understand the issue, take it upon yourself to explain the story and its vital details or background. Often, when a reporter fully understands your side of the story, initial hostilities will vanish. Even when no hostility exists, you will still enjoy an advantage when you present the facts accurately and in perspective.

4. *Do not try to manipulate the media.* The media know that people and organizations want to use these news outlets as a means of transmitting positive messages about themselves. Media people expect you to try to put your best foot forward. At the same time, they expect you to be honest with them. When the media perceive that you are trying to use them as unwitting accomplices in a self-serving scheme, they will tune you out and close their eyes and minds to your message. And, once you have abused your ties to the media, it is very difficult to rebuild their trust in you and what you have to say.

5. *Everything you say should be considered "on the record."* If you do not want to be quoted, say so immediately *before* speaking. Once reporters have identified themselves, they consider everything you say to be on the record, unless you both agree otherwise in advance.

If you say, "We're planning to build a new warehouse on property in the North Shore area, but that's off the record," the reporter is not ethically obliged to withhold that information from the story. First ask, "May we go off the record?" If the reporter agrees and you believe you are talking to someone you can trust, go ahead with your off-the-record comment. Be sure, however, that the reporter understands precisely what off the record means. And, as a source, be sure to indicate clearly when you are going back on the record. Understand, also, that if reporters obtain the material that you gave off the record from other sources who are willing to speak *for* the record, they are free to publish or broadcast it and to attribute it to those sources.

If the reporter refuses to agree to go off the record with you, you must decide whether to remain silent, speak for the record, or seek another alternative. One alternative is to speak "not for attribution" or "on deep background." When you speak for the record but not for attribution, it means that the information you provide will be used, but you will not be identified as its source.

When you read a news account that refers to "a senior State Department official who was not speaking for attribution," or "who was speaking for background only," you can surmise that the source is Secretary of State Suzannah Smart or someone very close to her. The secretary has decided that it is in her best interest to get the information out to the public but to do so in such a way that the report cannot be traced officially to her.

6. *Do not guess at answers when you do not have specific details at hand.* Offer to call back with the facts. It is good to set up the standards for your media relationships in advance. For instance, you might tell the reporters with whom you deal: "When I don't know the answers, I'll say so. When I find out the answers, I'll provide you with the information as soon

as possible." Once you have made that deal, live up to it. Also, do not guess at information about which you do not have expertise. Follow through by putting the reporter in touch with the right person.

7. *If you do not wish to discuss a particular subject, just say so.* Do not hem, haw, and obfuscate, and do not play twenty questions. When you allow reporters to pepper you with questions, they will gradually obtain enough information to enable them to infer the rest. It is not hard to say politely and firmly, "I repeat, I do not wish to discuss that subject."

8. *Be responsive to the reporter's need for information, but be sure to get your story across.* If questions seem to be going in a dead-end direction, take the lead and bring the subject back to more substantive matters.

9. *Take your time. Explain your views. Avoid jargon. Provide background.*

10. *Tell the truth.* Remember that what you are saying is going into the public record. You do not want your name to be associated with half-truths, exaggerations, and hyperbole. The reporter is probably relying on other sources as well as you, and the truth has a way of surfacing eventually. You can look foolish—and worse—if you come out on the wrong side of the truth. As a public person, realize that what you say becomes public record. As public record, it has an infinite life. Remember how long that is before you speak.

11. *Respect the competitive nature of media companies, which are private businesses.* If a reporter interviews you, do not then send out a news release with the same information to competing media.

12. *When you know about a pending story that the media will want to cover, inform them as soon as you*

can. Give the media as much lead time as possible. This will give them a chance to bone up on the information they need, sort out the complexities, understand the nuances, and decide how to write it and play it.

13. *If a story has an error, notify the reporter immediately and ask for a correction.* Remember: newspapers, audiotapes, and videotapes are historical records. In addition, the stories that appear in the newspaper and are electronically transmitted by radio and television will be filed in media reference libraries and computers. Each time another reporter uses a story for background, the erroneous information has a new life when it is incorporated in the current story. Ask that the correction be published or aired and that it be filed in the reference library along with the original story.

14. *Follow up when you do not think you have been treated fairly.* If you do not believe your side of an issue has been treated sufficiently, even if there are no published or broadcast errors of fact, do not hesitate to contact the media. You can work directly with the reporter to correct the story or do a follow-up piece; or you can request space or air time to respond to the story. As another alternative, especially appropriate with publications, you can write a letter to the editor or a longer essay to be considered as a "guest editorial." Address the letter or the essay to the editor of the editorial page. Remember to include your credentials that validate the credibility of your information.

15. *Remember that reporters are not editorial writers.* Editorials express the newspaper's or the station's formal position on an issue. Ordinarily, reporters play no role in shaping the policies of the editorial page or of

the station management. Often, they are as shocked and outraged at their newspaper's or station's editorial position as are any of the readers, listeners, or viewers. Editorial writers work independently of reporters, using the reporter's story only to gain factual information. If you attempt to "punish" the reporter for the sins of the editorial page, you might destroy a relationship that could, at some time, provide positive benefits for you and your organization.

When the Telephone Call Comes

You are sitting at your desk contemplating the success of your newest innovative product line when the telephone call comes. You recognize the throaty voice of Stella Telstar, the chief anchor on *Eyewitness News*.

"Mr. Jones," she says, "we've heard reports that the effluent from your plant is destroying the habitat of the Humboldt rockperch, a rare fish found only in the waters downstream from your plant. Could we talk to you about that on the air?"

Or it is the voice of Joe Muckraker, the investigative reporter for *The Daily Star and Telegraph*.

"Mr. Jones, we've heard that your board of directors just raised your CEO's salary to $750,000 a year plus stock options, right after she closed the plant in Mesquite Junction and put 600 people out of work. Can you explain how the company justifies this?"

The ball is now in your court, and you have to respond in a way that, if it does not enhance the image of your organization, will at least assure effective damage control.

Keep in mind the five basic intentions behind any interview you grant: (1) to persuade; (2) to instruct; (3) to inspire, (4) to activate; and (5) to entertain.

You want to *persuade* Ms. Telstar and her viewers that (a) the threat to the Humboldt rockperch is not coming from your plant; (b) if it is, your environmental experts are working, even as you speak, to eliminate the harmful effects so that the area can enjoy the economic benefits generated by your company while maintaining a pristine environment; or (c) the human benefits from your operation far outweigh the potential harm that might befall an obscure species of fish.

You want to *instruct* Mr. Muckraker and his readers about (a) the economic realities that forced the closure of the plant at Mesquite Junction; (b) how the policies of your CEO have resulted in a stronger, more competitive company that will safeguard the jobs of the remaining 30,000 employees; and (c) why the CEO's compensation package is what the company must pay to get an executive capable of leading it through the challenging times ahead.

You may *inspire* people by describing in uplifting terms the contributions your organization is making to the well-being of the community. You want to *motivate* people to *act* by encouraging people to get involved in your citizens' committee on environmental issues. And, if appropriate, you can *entertain* them through the use of disarming humor or engaging anecdotes that put your point across. Be careful, though, to keep your humor free of barbs that might alienate large numbers of people. Poking fun at the Humboldt rockperch may seem like a safe and easy thing to do, but if you utter ill-considered words, you might eventually have to eat them and, like the Humboldt rockperch, they may have bones.

Do not be intimidated by Stella Telstar or Joe Muckraker or any of their colleagues. Usually, they know less than you do about the story they are pursuing. That is why they are calling you—the expert. Approach the interview with the idea of helping them obtain the truth. When you are on the side of the truth, you can deal with people much more confidently.

Keep in mind the type of information a reporter is seeking. News consists of information that is timely. The more recent the event, the more newsworthy it is. Distinctiveness enhances news values. The more unusual an event, the more newsworthy. And news value grows with the number of people an event affects. Sometimes, the number of people indirectly affected has more bearing on newsworthiness than the number directly affected. When the missiles started raining on Baghdad at the outset of Desert Storm, the number of people directly affected was relatively small. But the outbreak of war had an indirect effect on the entire world.

Steps in Preparing for the Interview

You can take a number of steps to prepare yourself for an interview. First, when the news organization contacts you, make sure that you know which organization it is. Find out the reporter's name and *exactly* what the interview is about. Do not expect the reporter to tell you what questions you will be asked. Reporters usually let the information they are obtaining guide them in framing further questions.

Next, make sure that you are the appropriate person to be interviewed. If you are the human resource director and the reporter wants to interview you about chemical wastes, you probably should refer the call to your environmental department. Whatever the interview focus, if you do not know enough about the subject to discuss it, suggest someone else who might be able to help.

Prepare yourself with information you will need. Learn as much as you can about the story the reporter is working on. If the reporter calls out of the blue about an issue you have not anticipated, you might need to say, "Give me a few minutes to find out the facts, and I'll call you back."

If you know that the rockperch issue could surface, or if you have seen articles in the *Wall Street Journal* on the exorbitant earnings of corporate executives, prepare yourself in advance. You are likely to receive phone calls from Telstar and Muckraker. Prepare a mini-speech or "focus statement" on each subject you think the media might bring up. Focus on the issues or the core points you want to make. Prepare some pithy, accurate, quote-generating remarks that are on point—your point.

Try to anticipate the questions you will be asked, and have your answers ready. Say them aloud before you say them for the record. Develop a familiarity with your spoken response. Use this preparation as an opportunity to share thoughts you want the public to know.

A Congressman's Prepared Responses

As the press aide to Harry Reid, who served in the United States House of Representatives from Nevada before moving to the Senate, I was regularly called upon to prepare the congressman's response to major events. Here is the response we prepared to President Reagan's speech on the invasion of Grenada in 1983:

> I have four reasons to support the U.S. military participation in Grenada.
>
> First, it's clear that American lives were in danger. The twenty-four-hour curfew is strong evidence of the impending threat to the security of Americans in Grenada. Under this curfew, anyone who stepped outside the door would be shot on sight.
>
> Second, one prime minister was executed and his successor is missing. The succeeding ruler has proved to be violent and unpredictable.
>
> Third, it's obvious from reports, photographs, and eyewitness accounts that the island was being used as a Cuban military terrorist staging ground for controlling the rest of the Caribbean.
>
> And fourth, we were asked by the surrounding East Caribbean islands to participate in the military actions to regain the island.

Here is the response of Congressman Reid, a Democrat, to anticipated questions concerning the plans of

Republican Senator and National Committee Chairman Paul Laxalt to seek reelection in 1986:

> I've always accepted the fact that Senator Laxalt will be running for reelection in 1986. I say this for several reasons.
>
> One: President Reagan needs Senator Laxalt because it not only gives the president a close friend in the Senate, but also gives the president one more guaranteed Republican vote on key issues.
>
> Two: Senator Laxalt is chairman of the Republican Party and is necessary to the party as a political figurehead and as a party leader.
>
> Three: The senator has helped many Nevadans find high places in government, and they will continue to need him in the Senate.
>
> Four: Senator Laxalt has a viable opportunity to run for president or vice president, and this senatorial position provides him with ongoing visibility—a visibility with the current president.

Note how each of these responses focused on a few key points. In responding to the action in Grenada, Congressman Reid was stating clearly and succinctly his reasons for supporting the president. In his response to the question on Senator Laxalt, Reid took a carefully neutral position on the candidacy of his colleague from the other party. He found complimentary things to say about him, so that his response would not alienate the senator's supporters. But he also left himself the option of opposing Laxalt if the occasion arose. This type of careful response requires forethought. Incidentally, Laxalt decided not to run for reelection so he could run for president. Reid ran for and won Laxalt's vacated Senate seat in 1986. A footnote to history: Reid and Laxalt ran against each other for this same U.S. Senate seat in 1974. Reid lost that race by only 624 votes.

When You Need More Time

If you need time to collect your information and your thoughts, try to schedule the interview for a later date or time. Set a specific time and honor it. If you tell the reporter that you need time to prepare, you are giving assurance that you are willing to discuss the issue and that your answers will be well thought out.

Sometimes, though, the reporter will be unable to delay the interview. The deadline is *now*. The cameras or the presses will not wait. In such a situation, you have to deal with the information as truthfully and honestly as you can. Use pauses to gather your thoughts, and when you do respond, be brief, concise, and accurate. If you cannot produce all the information needed, be honest about it. Say, "I don't know the answer to that question right now; however, I can have it for you in a half-hour," or in whatever time period is appropriate. Set a timetable for delivering information, and do not extend your responses beyond what you are willing to handle. Follow through with your deadline even if you do not have the expected answers. Make that call to update the reporter. In fact, call sooner if you can.

Principles for Dealing with the Public and the Media

Since 1964, I have worked with high-visibility people who want to make positive connections with their communities, which can be defined geographically, economically, professionally, and in numerous other ways. Following are several principles that will help you when you deal with the public (the examples have been disguised to protect the identity of clients):

- **Be willing to share your goals, objectives, and standards.** Consider this example of a sales manager telling a reporter for a business magazine how he goes about recruiting people for his sales team:

> Recruiting is still the main key to having a successful enterprise. I don't care what type of program you have, you need to have quality people to be successful. We look first for the great salesperson, and then we look to see if that person will fit in—socially, emotionally, and culturally—at Cosmic Technologies. Our salespeople have to be highly motivated, because Cosmic is a quality company and they have to work hard to continue advancing.

This was an excellent response. It hit all the key elements that pertain to salespeople: quality, great salesperson, emotionally and culturally balanced, and highly motivated. It was a good pitch about the company's standards and a terrific synopsis of goals and objectives.

- **Do not speak for other people.** Note this example from the comment of a chief environmental officer responding to reports that the Environmental Protection Agency was investigating her company's compliance with regulations regarding sulfur dioxide emissions:

> I understand that SO_2 is no more than 20 percent of what they're dealing with. Our SO_2 emissions opened the door, and they stepped through the door and are allowing themselves a long look at the whole range of emissions.

The environmental officer was feeding the media raw red meat with this response. The question had focused on the investigation into sulfur dioxide. Why expand the response into other areas? And why serve as a spokesperson for the EPA? A fair and accurate response would have been, "The EPA is looking into our sulfur dioxide emissions. We're cooperating fully with the investigation." Had the reporter asked for details of the findings, the appropriate response would have been, "The investigation continues. I cannot address the details. You'll need to talk to the EPA."

- **Do not taint your own credibility.** Here is a comment from a labor negotiator for a privately held company on the union's demands for a total restructuring of wages and benefits based on the company's recent earnings:

> I've said from the very beginning, once we created an opening—once we granted them access to our books—that they

> would rummage through our files to exam-
> ine anything that bore on our financial
> strength. In my opinion, their demands
> have escalated.

"I've said from the beginning" is an unnecessary disclaimer. You do not need to remind reporters of something you said long ago. It is not up to you to refresh their memories unless the reminder is relevant to the quote. What was the purpose in reconfirming a long-held negative position with the language "rummage through our files?" Same goes for "In my opinion." Avoid volunteering opinions that make a negative position look worse. And you certainly do not want to flag the audience that you are insecure about what you are saying.

- **Provide quotes that you can live with beyond the moment.** Consider this quote from a frustrated CEO responding to the questions of a persistent reporter who wanted to know the real reasons for firing a popular vice president who had been active in civic affairs:

> You can say we're a heartless bunch of
> ingrates if you want to. I don't want to
> comment on the real reason.

Whatever piqued the CEO, he needs to remember that he cannot let his emotions overwhelm him at a time when he is expected to demonstrate stability.

- **Avoid negative approaches.** Note this one used by the campaign director for a United Way drive:

> I don't think we'll have any trouble meeting
> our goals for this campaign. At least, I
> hope not.

Why preface your positive statement with "I don't think," and why qualify it with "At least, I hope not?" State it positively: "I'm confident we'll meet or exceed our campaign goals."

- Avoid singling out particular persons for public comment, whether positive or negative. Study this comment from a basketball coach about a player who had played a brilliant game but had remarked that he was still "feeling down" after committing some mental errors in a previous contest:

> Isn't he a great kid? When do you ever hear a player talk about a bad game after having a game like he had tonight? He's such a sensitive kid. I don't know where you will ever find a better kid.

It is uplifting for a coach to praise a star player, but it can be overdone. How do the other players feel when they read that their coach does not "know where you will ever find a better kid?" The comment could cause rivalries and resentment among the players.

- Do not "pass the buck" for responsibility when people consider you to be the person in power. Note these words of a CEO explaining why construction of a needed waste-treatment plant fell behind schedule:

> I'm not too happy with our construction schedule, but that's how it worked out. The EPA standards for our effluent are particularly stringent. Just when we had hoped to begin letting bids, our engineers decided to go a different route on treat-

> ment methods. Then we ran into some
> bad weather in early December and that
> threw us behind. If we could just get those
> EPA standards down to a reasonable level
> it would make things easier on all of us.

That statement makes the CEO and his company appear indecisive and incapable. Saying "but that's how it worked out" gives the impression that the CEO had no part in the mechanics of scheduling. It dilutes his position of authority over the construction project. The engineers work for him; why were they permitted to make that last-minute change in treatment methods? In most places, bad weather is a common occurrence in early December. Why wasn't that taken into account in the scheduling? And why use EPA rules as a scapegoat when everyone else in your business is expected to live by the same regulations?

Good power communications would have resulted in a response like this:

> We are behind schedule. Fortunately, the
> extra time buys us an extra margin of
> environmental protection. Just as we were
> ready to go to bids, we discovered a new,
> more effective method of waste treat-
> ment and we decided to take that route.
> That route required some extra time
> because we improved our engineering
> plans. It also meant rolling the dice with
> the weather in December. We knew,
> though, that our decision would reap
> great benefits—like clean water. We'll
> continue to meet or exceed EPA stan-

> dards for water quality—which are quite
> high. That's our commitment to our proj-
> ect and the community we serve.

- **You can experience long-term effects by denying access to the media.** You might have problems later when you want the media to listen. Certainly, at times, you might want to walk away from reporters, refuse to return their calls, and hang up with a "no comment" when they call, and you have that right. In so doing, however, you are laying the groundwork for one-sided stories that portray you and your organization in a negative light. The reporter's justification for this: "Every time I tried to reach you to get your side of the story, you were never available."

- **Do not anticipate someone else's decision.** Note this response from the head of a governmental agency whose subordinates were under investigation for irregularities in the use of public funds:

> Unless they plan to drop a big bomb on me
> during the next two visits, I don't believe
> we have any major violations. They have
> uncovered secondary violations. The mis-
> use of department telephones, the per-
> sonal use of government automobiles, and
> charging parking tickets on expense
> accounts we've already admitted to.

First, the administrator must remember that she is speaking as a *spokesperson*. Therefore, what she says as the person in authority becomes *fact* in the minds of the public. This imposes upon spokespersons a heavy responsibility to weigh their words before speaking them. By second-guessing what might happen, the head of the agency has set herself up for a fall. Her remarks taunt the investigators. If the examiners are set on finding something, the administrator should not tell the world publicly, via the media, that they are *not* going to do something. They will just redouble their efforts to prove her wrong, and they may actually surprise her. If the investigators do turn up more major violations, nobody will remember that the administrator qualified her statement with the words "I don't believe." People will simply conclude that she was caught on the wrong side of the truth.

Also note that the agency head referred to some infractions "we've already admitted to." This sounds as though she actually revealed this information against her will. Be careful about such negative assertions and, generally, avoid over-responding with details. If you do make remarks about the admission, merely say, "The Government Accounting Office has noted the misuse of. . . ."

- **Say only what you know and can support.** Here is what the head of a Chamber of Commerce economic development task force had to say about an industrial prospect:

> We're optimistic about bringing a new industry with 300 jobs into the community. I've been told that we've made the final cut and are at the top of the list of possible locations. I feel 95 percent sure that the company will relocate here, but we won't know for certain until Monday.

Avoid making statements until you can support them. When you say, "I've been told . . ." you are passing your quote off to some vague person from somewhere else, and acknowledging that you are not sure about what you are saying. If you are not sure, then do not say it. Do not make statements until you know the information is true. In this case, the task force head should have stopped after the first sentence.

- **Be careful about "setting up" future events with negative language.** These were the comments of the manager of a newly opened industrial plant:

> This is going to be a tough year for us. Our management team and employees have never worked together before and they're going to be operating in a new environment and with new and unfamiliar equipment. We expect some production glitches. It'll probably take us a while to get quality up to where we want it to be. But I think we'll be fine by the first of November.

Be careful about setting up your organization, the media, and the public for such negative performance, especially in such specific terms. The negative expectations often become self-fulfilling prophecies.

- **Mention "concerns" briefly, in the most positive way possible.** Then, in an equally positive way, move on to other points, including your plans to resolve these concerns. Note this statement by an incumbent politician, responding to his controversial position on abortion:

> This is a race in which records of accomplishment will make the difference. I recognize that we might take different positions on some issues. However, during my eight years in office, I've successfully introduced vital legislation on education, health care, tax relief, and other crucial consumer issues. I've listened to the people and delivered legislative answers to their concerns.

Well done. The candidate knew he faced a tough race, yet he answered from a position of his strength. This approach surpasses saying that the opposition is "scary," or that the candidate is "worried" and "running scared." The statement ends on a note of strength and responsiveness.

- **Do not knowingly give false information.** Consider the way a municipal public works director handled it when asked whether asbestos pipes were still being used in the municipal water system:

> I can only tell you about the asbestos that has been installed since 1976. I know that we haven't installed asbestos pipes since I came to this job in 1981. At that time, some of the pipes were already in the ground. Up until that time, record-keeping was spotty. Our environmental experts confirm that if asbestos pipes are there, they present minimal health hazards. We continually test the water for asbestos fibers. So far, none of the tests has shown a significant amount of asbestos in the test samples.

Note that the director does not categorically deny the existence of asbestos pipes in the system. He tells what he knows and he tells what he has done about the situation. He avoids guessing. On the question of test results, he cites what he knows up to this point. If subsequent research proves him wrong, nobody can fault him. He has spoken about what he knows, not what he presumes or predicts.

- **Do not reaffirm the negative language others proffer.** For example, a top corporate official made this statement:

> Everybody says we're union busters, but we're not the only ones picking fights. The union bosses have opposed every move we've tried to make to improve efficiency and productivity. They've fought us at the bargaining table, they've fought us on the picket lines, and they've fought us with lies and distortions in the media. Well, we can play that game too. If they want to fight dirty, we'll get down and fight dirty with them, and we can be just as mean as they can.

That quote should never have been uttered. It is completely negative and potentially destructive. It opens too many doors to future criticism. If he needed to make such a statement, the official should not have reaffirmed the negative language initiated by others. Why repeat the accusation that the company is a union-buster? By restating it, the corporate official gave the negative language a second generation of public exposure. If you must challenge the

integrity of other persons, do not follow up by saying, "We can play that game too." This leaves you
completely open to the accusation that you have no
integrity either. Your last words are heard the loud-
est, and what were this official's last words? "We'll
get down and fight dirty with them, and we can be
just as mean as they can."

Carefully select the language you use when you
are speaking for the public record. The executive
could have made the statement simply: "We'll fight
hard for the legitimate interests of this corporation
and its employees, whether the challenge comes
from the competition or from the union."

- **Do not perpetuate negative language and stories.**
  Learn how to "let go." Politician A had accused Politician B of illegal use of campaign contributions
  following a hard-fought election. An investigation
  failed to turn up enough evidence to support the
  charges, and Politician A apologized. As a new campaign began to develop, with the two candidates
  again pitted as opponents, Politician B was asked
  how he felt about the accusation now. His response:

  > I don't really want to get into that too
  > much. I want the people involved in our
  > campaign to come out and work hard.
  > What he said is not forgotten. You can't
  > forgive a guy for coming out on the record
  > and saying what he said about me last
  > year.

The opponent took a more positive, responsible
approach with his statement:

I've had some time to think about it and I feel badly about what I said, even though at the time I thought I was right. I've apologized to him, both publicly and privately, and will *do whatever's equitable to reconcile our differences.*

One of the most difficult disciplines we need to develop is that of experiencing pain and moving beyond that pain. We need to learn how to *turn setbacks (or challenges) into opportunities.* You cannot make the past go away. However, you certainly can damage your future by perpetuating the negative past. Although the investigation had not produced hard facts to support the charges, the accusation itself had raised questions in the minds of many voters. By pricking at old wounds, Politician B kept the issue alive. Politician A stuck to the high road on this occasion, and was rewarded on election day. Incidentally, he had learned a valuable lesson: timely public apologies can enhance credibility.

Politician B would have been better served had he simply responded: "Those charges have been investigated and laid to rest, my opponent has apologized, I've accepted his apologies, and I'd prefer to move on to more important issues."

- **Use a prepared statement when the situation is volatile and a poor choice of words could trigger a debacle.** Prepared statements can also help you when a person or your organization gets involved in controversy and your spokesperson does not want to speak directly to the media. I used this approach with a college basketball player. During the last seven seconds of a heated game, he punched an opposing player after which a major fight broke out between the teams. The incident received national attention, and the player's behavior definitely called for a public response. He did not want to face the media, and, in the emotionally charged atmosphere, there was a good chance that he would say something to worsen the situation. I worked with his coach to craft a prepared statement:

> I'm very sorry about what happened. I had nine stitches in my mouth from an injury at practice two days ago. The same player—who knew about my injury—hit me in the mouth three times in the game. Each time he hit me, I hurt a little more. I was in the kind of pain that provoked me to react. Leaving the court, I was surrounded by their players. There was a lot of anger going both ways. Again, I'm very sorry this all happened.

The media generally do not like prepared statements, but they will use them if that is all they can get. By confining the response to the prepared statement, we created the first and last word from the player.

Even when it is necessary to confront the media in person, you do not have to do so unprepared. It is usually possible to anticipate 80 to 90 percent of the questions in advance and to prepare responses to them. Being prepared enables you to go into the situations with more comfort and confidence.

- **Be careful about making yourself a self-appointed spokesperson for others.** A chamber of commerce president attended a regional meeting at which a proposal surfaced for a joint economic development agency to bring new payrolls into the region. The region consisted of several municipalities of similar size. Approached by a reporter following the meeting, the enthusiastic president said:

> I think I can speak for everyone in my organization in saying that this plan will result in phenomenal growth for our area and that we're 100 percent behind it.

The proposal died because individual members of his chamber of commerce opposed it. They feared that the proposal would give other localities the upper hand in attracting business to their particular cities. The chamber president had presumed to speak for members of his organization, without checking to determine what they thought about the proposal. A more prudent approach would have been to say: "The proposal certainly looks good to me, and I personally could support it enthusiastically. However, as you know, the chamber of commerce represents the entire business community in our city, and I'm not in a position to speak for every one of its individual members."

- **Avoid pointing fingers at the media.** The media, like all other institutions, have their warts and their feet of clay. They also have something else: the last word. Antagonizing the media or blaming misfortunes on the media will usually bring counterproductive results to you. Vice President Spiro Agnew's characterization of the media as "nattering nabobs of negativism" was repeated often and gleefully by the media themselves, with no enhancement to the vice president's image. Again, the media had the last word.

• **Make your last impression your best impression.** In the sports arena, NBA star Larry Johnson, while a student at the University of Nevada-Las Vegas, was an excellent practitioner of this technique. I media-coached Johnson and his teammates for two years about the importance of their *words* and their *actions* in making positive impressions. After one hard-fought contest, Johnson shook the hands of several opponents, and even put his arm around their shoulders. The action left a parting impression of good sportsmanship. No wonder the community named Johnson its most popular athlete.

The media can be cantankerous, arbitrary, capricious, unpredictable, and sometimes downright mean. But in the aggregate, the media provide an invaluable conduit for those who need to convey information and project images to the public. Equally important, the media serve a crucial role in perpetuating democracy.

Thomas Jefferson felt the scurrilous sting of the press of his day, but the great egalitarian was moved to write in the year the Constitution was adopted:

> Were it left for me to decide whether we should have a government without newspapers, or newspapers without a government, I should not hesitate a moment to prefer the latter.

Had there been radio and television in his time, he surely would have included them in his preference.

In Summary:

• When you become a public person, the media will seek you out, even when you would prefer not to make a public statement.

• The fifteen standard rules for interacting with the media are:

   1. When a reporter or other media person calls, take the call.
   2. Return the call immediately or as soon as possible on the day the call comes in.
   3. Be thorough, yet brief.
   4. Do not try to manipulate the media.
   5. Everything you say should be considered "on the record."
   6. Do not guess at answers when you do not have specific details at hand.
   7. If you do not wish to discuss a particular subject, say so.
   8. Be responsive to the reporter's need for information, but be sure to get your story across.
   9. Take your time. Explain your views. Avoid jargon. Provide background.
   10. Tell the truth.
   11. Respect the competitive nature of media companies, which are private businesses.
   12. When you know about a pending story that the media will want to cover, inform them as soon as you can.
   13. If a story has an error, notify the reporter immediately and ask for a correction.
   14. Follow up when you do not think you have been treated fairly.

15. Remember that reporters are not editorial writers.

- Your basic purpose in speaking through the media is to persuade, instruct, inspire, activate, and entertain.

- Take these steps in preparing for an interview:

    1. Make sure that you know which organization is asking for your comments.
    2. Find out the reporter's name and *exactly* what the interview is to be about.
    3. Make sure you are the appropriate person to be interviewed. If you are not, suggest someone who is.
    4. Find out as much as you can about the story the reporter is working on. Ask the reporter for time to obtain the information. Then obtain all the facts you can about it.
    5. Prepare a mini-speech, or "focus statement," on each subject you think the media might bring up. Focus on the issues or the core points you want to make.
    6. Try to anticipate the questions you will be asked, and have your answers ready. Say them aloud *before* you say them for the record.

- Keep these principles in mind as you deal with the media:

    1. Be willing to share your goals, objectives, and standards.
    2. Do not speak for other people unless you are specifically designated to do so; even then, know to what extent you can speak for them.

3. Do not taint your own credibility.
4. Provide quotes that you can live with beyond the moment.
5. Avoid negative approaches.
6. Be careful about singling out particular persons for public comment, whether positive or negative.
7. Do not "pass the buck" for responsibility when people consider you to be the "expert" or the one in power. Remember, though, that if you are not the expert, then you should pass the interview on to the person who can address the subject authoritatively.
8. If you deny the media ready access to you, you might have problems later when you want the media to listen.
9. Say only what you can support.
10. Be careful about "setting up" future events with negative language.
11. When talking about a "concern," refer to the concern briefly in a positive way. Then move on to other positive points, including the way you plan to resolve your concerns.
12. Do not reaffirm or perpetuate others' negative language, premises, or stories.
13. Use a prepared statement when a situation is volatile and a poor choice of words could trigger a debacle.
14. Avoid pointing fingers at the media.
15. Make your last impression your best impression.

8

How to Master the Interview

One of the stiffest challenges for the public person is the media interview. You are on the spot, with a skilled questioner intent on getting the story the media want, and not necessarily the one that you want to convey. When faced with this situation, regard it as an opportunity to get your message across. When the interview is on radio or television, you have a chance to reach a large audience *directly* with *your* message. Be prepared to seize the opportunity.

To turn the interview to your advantage, take control. You do not have to reveal any information you choose not to reveal, nor do you have to answer questions you prefer not to answer. Put simply, say only what you want to say. In fact, the interview environment provides you with the ideal opportunity to give the answers *you* want to give and the information *you* want to impart.

Most interviewers do not intend to entangle you in your own words. Nor do they set out to make you look awkward or feel embarrassed. You can help yourself and the interviewer by working toward a friendly, relaxed relationship *before* the interview. Let's take a look at ways in which you can use your power communications to reap substantial benefits from the television interview. Remember: on television, you convey your total message not only by what you say but also by how you say it—with your voice and with your body language.

When you are being interviewed for a televised newscast, you can begin the interview process by suggesting an appropriate setting for your interaction with the media. Generally, this location should provide a visual background for the story. For example, if you are going to explain your company's efforts in behalf of literacy, you might select an elementary school with a classroom of first-graders reading aloud in the background. If you are going to be explaining your organization's efforts in behalf of the homeless, you might choose a homeless shelter, or you might take the interviewer to the section of town where the homeless congregate.

Be sure that the location you select is quiet so that background noises do not compete with your efforts to get your message across to the reporter and the ultimate audience. Meaningful interviews can be difficult to conduct, especially for radio or television, when the noise from other people or activities are intrusive.

Preparing for the Interview

Once you have scheduled the interview, move forward with the rest of your preparations. If you are not already familiar with the program and with the interviewer, watch it, observe its format, and note what people being interviewed are expected to provide.

From the outset, you should know the general subject to be discussed. You are already conversant with it, at least in generalities, or the producer or editor would not want to interview you. On camera, you want to be well versed in specifics as well. Do your homework until you "own" the subject and can produce specific information spontaneously and naturally.

Prepare "focus statements"—eighty words or less— that summarize key points you want to make. These statements can provide you with ready answers to friendly questions and, as we shall see later, they can help you negotiate mine fields of hostile questions.

As an expert on your subject, anticipate the questions you are likely to be asked. To fortify yourself, think of the toughest questions the interviewer could ask you and write those questions down in the most negative possible language. Once you have decided how you want to respond, write down the answers. Rehearse your responses out loud and continue practicing them in a relaxed, conversational manner. The key here is to develop a response that is accurate, comfortable, and easy for you to communicate in the spoken, not written, language. You will also need to include anecdotes or other support data to reinforce your points.

I recommended this approach to a high-profile elected official during an intensive media-training program I presented to political leaders. "How do you feel when you see reporters approaching you with lights on and cameras rolling?" I asked him.

"I wonder what they're going to do to me," he responded.

To ease his discomfort, I gave him a daily exercise: write down the worst-case-scenario questions about pending legislation that you might be asked; then craft the answers you are willing to see on the front page of tomorrow's newspaper.

"I'd rather give 'spontaneous answers,' " he said.

"That's fine," I told him. "But do this exercise just once. And remember, the first word you scratch out in that prepared response is the second chance you don't get with the media when you improvise your answers."

In addition to the interview scenario, this same preparation will help you with speaking events, public presentations, and other high-profile comunications opportunities.

Dressing for the Interview

For simplicity and focus, I will give you several pointers on dressing for television because how you look is especially important with this medium. So, before you leave for the interview, make sure you are dressed appropriately for the occasion. Under ordinary circumstances, a business suit is fine. When the interview is conducted in your work setting, however, you can wear the clothes you would ordinarily wear at work.

If you are going to participate in a formal television interview, you will want to pay special attention to what you wear. For men, medium to dark solid-color suits are best. Steer away from stark black-and-white combinations. Solid-color shirts, especially lighter pastels, look better than white, and do not wear shirts with narrow stripes because they tend to "move" on camera. Burgundy and red ties show up well on television; however, whatever the color, select a tie that is tasteful. And if you decide to wear a patterned suit, shirt, or tie, avoid wearing more than two patterns at the same time, and be sure that the patterns you select do not compete with one another. Wear dark socks that cover the calves and avoid wing-tip shoes because they look too heavy on television; light slip-on shoes are best.

For women, skirted suits or dresses with jackets in medium or dark tones work well, though more and more executives are wearing jewel tones. Dresses or blouses look best on camera when they are deep, warm tones and without extravagant patterns. Blouses may be red, warm pink, apricot, peach, or other pastels, not stark white.

Even though fashion might herald flamboyant blouses, short skirts, and wild accessories, the public person should remember that fashion is not necessarily appropriate when you are being interviewed about important issues. Therefore, when assembling your television attire, remember that your blouse should be conservatively designed so that it does not detract the viewers' attention from what you are saying. Your skirt should cover the knees. You should keep your jewelry to a minimum and, if you do wear jewelry, choose accessories that do not compete with the image you want to convey. For example, wear pearls or nonglittering stones. Especially avoid glittery lapel pins because these become visual focal points and distract the eye. Neutral-toned hosiery and shoes with closed toes look best for television.

Build Rapport with the Interviewer

Work at building a rapport with the interviewer. While the camera crew is setting up, engage in a friendly but purposeful dialogue. Find out what the interview will involve so that you can mentally prepare yourself for the questions. Do not ask for special treatment regarding particularly sensitive issues because interviewers like to control their own questions; the interviewer might be inclined to delve into the very areas you had hoped to avoid.

Getting to know the interviewer will help you feel more comfortable by the time the camera operator signals you that you are being videotaped or are on the air. Your goal when on camera is to strike a workable balance between nervous energy and lethargy. Let your energy and expertise work for you.

Just before the interview, you will want to remember a few pointers. Start with a good night's sleep the night before your interview; this will help you face the interview in top physical and mental condition. Mental rehearsal is a good way to prepare yourself for what is to come, and it helps minimize your nervousness.

A group of basketball players once was divided into three groups. One group practiced its shooting in the gym for twenty minutes every day for a month. It improved its shooting percentage by about 24 percent. Another group did no actual practicing. Instead, its members mentally pictured themselves making the perfect shots. They increased their shooting percentage by 23 percent. Members of the third group did not practice in the gym and did not practice in their minds. Their shooting percentage did not improve.

The experiment showed that mental rehearsal is just about as effective as actual rehearsal. These visualization techniques can help you in many ways. Before you show up for the interview, and even while you are waiting for the cameras to start, envision yourself in the interview situation. See yourself taking the questions you have anticipated in advance and confidently and calmly delivering the answers you have prepared.

Use the minutes leading up to the interview to organize your thoughts. Think in small, organized chunks of information. Put ideas in perspective. Sure, this interview is important, or you would not be here. Do not let it overwhelm you, though, because this interview provides just one piece to a much larger picture. Again, remind yourself that this interview will provide you with an opportunity to share important ideas.

Another tip to reroute nervousness: focus your attention outward, toward the other people on the scene. Chat with the interviewer and the camera crew. This will help you develop more control over your anxieties. If you find yourself tensing up when the crew attaches your microphone just prior to the beginning of the interview, take two or three deep breaths, inhale through the nose, and exhale through the mouth. Slowly fill your lungs to their full capacity. Then, slowly breathe all the way out. While you are doing this, concentrate on nothing but breathing. This exercise immediately drops your body's lactate levels that foster your stress. Put yourself in a positive mood and remind yourself: "Finally, a chance to tell *my* side of this story. I will not be intimidated; I am in control."

Listen Carefully

The media interview is an especially appropriate time to practice your good listening skills. It is important that you listen carefully to everything everybody says and the way they phrase statements and questions. Do not respond to and do not repeat erroneous phrasing. You will want to listen not only to what is said, but also *how* it is said. Take note of sarcasm, levity, and other emotions that accompany the words. Do not let an uncivil manner goad you into an uncivil response. You remain in control when you maintain your dignity and aplomb. Give a polite and invigorating response and move on.

Be sure that you are responding to what the interviewer has said, and not to what you *assumed* would be said. This requires careful, attentive listening. The importance of this was doubly emphasized at a power-presentation seminar I conducted several years ago.

One of the attendees of that seminar had recently participated in a three-person panel discussion focused on customer service. She had been the middle presenter. I had been in the audience and remembered what the third presenter had said on the subject of listening. I asked the participant in my seminar to share with our audience what she had heard. She said she had not heard it; she had sat through the first speaker's presentation in numb anticipation, and had sat through the third speaker's delivery in numb relief.

Had she paid attention to the third panelist, she would have heard a story that underscored the point about listening. A prominent celebrity appeared on one of the late-night talk shows. The host, with a smile, asked his guest how her life was going. The guest responded that her mother had died earlier that week. Without a blink, the host laughed and said, "That's great to hear." My seminar participant could have learned a valuable lesson about listening—had she only listened.

Sometimes, no matter how closely you listen, you may not be sure what the interviewer means by certain questions. When the question is subject to misunderstanding, you should repeat it, perhaps paraphrasing for clarity. This assures that you are answering the right question and that the interviewer and audience know which question you are answering.

Use your own judgment when you think the interviewer is using the question as a platform to advance a personal position. Take control of the situation: "You've provided me with a lot of information. Let's see if this is what you're asking. . . ." Having phrased the question to your liking, give a brief answer that includes *your* point.

When faced with hostile statements, remember your focus points—those brief statements you have prepared in advance to portray your position concisely, clearly, and accurately. If you do not want to answer the question as asked, "bridge" or "re-direct" to a focus point.

Responding to Difficult Questions

When responding to difficult questions, back up your answers with authority. You can cite your own professional experience or your own personal experience. Another alternative is to quote experts or present undisputed or documentable facts. You might choose to disassociate from the issue with a statement such as "That's like comparing carbon sheets to parchment paper."

You can often defuse hostility by establishing a bond with the interviewer and bridging to the point you want to make: "I can certainly understand why you would think that, Jane. Let me explain why we used that approach. . . ." If you do not know the answer to a question, do not try to fake it. It is okay to say, "I don't know. I will look into that matter and let you know what I learn."

And remember, although you have consented to the interview, you have not agreed to open to the interviewer every aspect of your life. You do not have to answer personal questions that are unrelated to your profession or the reason you are being interviewed. You also do not have to answer questions that involve litigation or a process that might be compromised by your comment.

Basic Types of Questions

Your interviewer will use four basic types of questions:

1. *The Yes-No Question.* This is an efficient way of getting to the basic information, but it does not give you a ready opening for more extensive dialogue.
2. *The Closed Question.* This is used when the interviewer wants precise information. The question usually begins with words such as *when, where, who,* and *what.*
3. *The Open-Information Question.* This is often used to encourage longer responses and more information. Such questions often begin with the words *how, why,* and *what.*
4. *Unstructured Beginnings.* These questions often begin with phrases such as "tell me about . . ." or "describe for us. . . ." Such questions encourage you to think and express your thoughts and emotions. They also are strong rapport-builders, increasing your comfort level and enabling you and the interviewer to deal more directly and completely.

The interviewer's questions will appeal to you in one of three ways:

1. Questions you *can* answer and *want* to answer.
2. Questions you *can* answer and would *rather not* answer, directly or indirectly.
3. Questions you *cannot* answer.

Henry Kissinger, the former secretary of state and national security adviser, was one of the most successful exploiters of communication opportunities. Once, during a news conference, he asked, "Does anyone have questions for my answers?"

Kissinger realized that a news conference or an interview provided more than an environment for mere questions and answers; it also created an opportunity for delivering prepared statements on matters he wanted to discuss.

Responding to the questions you can answer and want to answer will be easy if you have prepared your brief focus statements.

Responding to questions you cannot answer can also be simple. You do it in three words: "I don't know." Having said that, you should follow up with action and a timetable for that action. Again, just remember that you never want to fake an answer. Nothing destroys your credibility faster than fabricating a response.

Dealing with questions you can answer, but would rather not, requires a bit more skill. When you handle difficult questions correctly, however, you can use them as opportunities to stress points you want to make.

The Answer Plus Supporting Data

Remember that your purpose in granting the interview is to impart information. It should be the information *you* want to share and to the extent you want to share it.

Your best response to a question provides the answer plus one piece of support data. Your support may be a reason, a justification, a statistic, a quotation, or a fact. If you want to hint that there is more information where that came from, flag your response with qualifiers, such as *primary, main, most essential,* and *major,* as in:

> Our *primary focus* . . .
> The *most important reason for* . . .
> The *company's major concern* . . .

Alert interviewers will pick up on these words and ask follow-up questions.

If You're Not Happy with the Question. . . .

If you do not like the way a question is phrased, ask the interviewer to repeat it. This gives the interviewer a chance to hear the question again. If it is repeated precisely the way it was phrased the first time, you know that the interviewer is determined to use the same language and, sometimes, trying to make you uncomfortable.

If you are not happy with the way the interviewer

phrases a question, you might try phrasing it yourself. Ask your own question. This shows a legitimate interest in the question. It also helps you to focus it and narrow it to a more specific or precise point.

You can also ask for clarification of the question. This forces the interviewer to refine the question. When your interviewer uses terms that might be subject to more than one interpretation, ask for definitions. This keeps you and the interviewer from operating from different perspectives and biases. It is not necessary that you both agree on a definition. You just want to be sure that you both know which definition is being used.

At times, you will encounter questions you would rather not answer directly, or would prefer not to answer in their entirety. You would prefer to move on to other topics. Skillful *sidestepping* will enable you to get around the question while remaining in control and maintaining credibility. Suppose you get a question like this:

> Is it true that the line of vacuum cleaners manufactured in your local plant has been plagued by problems involving poor quality, and that you're going to stop making them here and begin marketing a Japanese product instead?

Obviously, this question is sensitive. You are talking about the possibility of closing a local plant, eliminating local jobs, and exporting the payroll to Japan. You are also dealing with the implication that your product is inferior and that you are blaming the local employees for its problems. The interviewer has hit close to the truth, but you are not ready to announce anything yet. How do you sidestep the question?

One technique is to respond to only one aspect of the question. You might reply:

> For some time we've been considering the possibility of affiliating with a Japanese company in some sort of joint venture. We've been in touch with one company that manufactures a product similar to ours. By working together, we know we can learn some things from them and they can learn from us.

With this technique, you have answered the part of the question that deals with the Japanese connection. Note, though, that you have not repeated, or responded to, the part that deals with poor quality and the prospect of exporting jobs.

Another technique is to *refocus* the question. To do this, you take one word from the question—not one that involves the sensitive concept—and build a strong, supported response around it. Your response to the question might be:

> We're certainly looking at the marketing side of our business. We realize that the key to success in the global marketplace is to find out what customers want and give it to them. So we're looking at what products we might want to market in the future and how best we can provide them for our customers.

In this case, you have taken the word "marketing" from the question and have focused the response on that word. You have not touched on the Japanese or the poor-quality angle.

Finally, you can *bridge* or *re-direct* the question. This technique helps you move smoothly from the interviewer's point to the point you want to make. You can bridge any time the interviewer has asked you a question you would rather not answer directly. The key is to use a transitional statement, then go to one of the focus statements you have prepared in advance.

The transitional statement involves the interviewer by acknowledging the value of the original question. Once you have accomplished this, you can move on to your focus statement. An example of how this works follows:

> *Acknowledgment of reporter's question:* "Our company has been studying several options to fine-tune our operations." (Pause)
> *Bridging statement:* "Let me tell you about our new marketing strategy."
> *Focus statement:* "We have created a five-point program to reach national and international customers. . . ."

Other examples of this technique are:

> "That's an interesting point." (Pause) "The central issue here is. . . ." *Focus statement.*
>
> "That was true last year." (Pause) "This year we're concentrating on. . . ." *Focus statement.*
>
> "We're looking into that." (Pause) "We're also considering. . . ." *Focus statement.*

Remember to keep your focus statements short. The listening span for most people is thirty seconds or less. That is why television advertisers make such extensive use of the thirty-second commercial, and many are now turning to ten-second versions. If your answer runs on much longer than ten to twenty seconds, your audience will drift.

Tricky Questions

Some questions will be tricky and they may even be deliberately designed to trip you up. Such questions become easier to handle, though, when you know the different types and learn to deal with each. Here are some of them:

1. *The A-or-B dilemma.* "Ms. Executive, we understand that a new pollution-control device is available that would greatly increase the air quality in our area if you were to install it at your old plant. Do you plan to spend millions of dollars for this device, or will you continue to pollute our air?"

Never opt for the choices given if neither of them is correct. Your answer to that question might be:

> We're interested in anything that might improve the quality of the air in this area. After all, we breathe it, too. Fortunately, our old plant already is equipped with state-of-the-art equipment, and meets every relevant standard for emission control. You might be interested in knowing that the air quality in this area is well

> above the norm for metropolitan areas of
> this size, and that the heaviest contribu-
> tor to air pollution here is the automobile
> exhaust pipe.

2. *Irrelevant questions.* If the question is totally off base, say you do not understand it and bridge to the key point you want to make—your focus statement. Let's say you are spearheading a drive to build a new municipally owned conference center for your city. Your interviewer observes:

> The homeless situation in this city is
> growing daily. People are sleeping on
> street gratings. What will your convention
> center do for them?

You might answer:

> The convention center doesn't relate
> directly to the homeless situation.
> (Pause) Let me tell you, though, what the
> center will do for our city's economy. . . .

3. *Absent-party questions.* Do not speak for other people. You are not in a position to know why other people do or say certain things, so be cautious about responding as though you do. Even when you are a spokesperson for another person or organization, be careful about the extent to which you can speak for them. Your interviewer observes:

> The mayor has staked her prestige on
> approval of the bond referendum to
> finance the new center. What do you think
> she will do if the referendum fails?

Do not yield to the temptation to speak for the mayor. Simply answer, with a smile: "That's a question you need to ask the mayor."

4. *The inconsistency trap.* If your position has changed over time, be prepared to explain why it changed. Do not expect to maintain credibility if you make a practice of switching positions. You can switch once per issue, based on your discovery of new information, or on a change in circumstances. The interviewer says:

> Five years ago, as a representative of the neighborhood association, you fought against a home for unwed mothers near the Elmwood Forest subdivision. You claimed that it would disturb the quiet residential environment. Now that you're no longer a resident, you're advocating the establishment on that same site of a social services office building, which would attract a great deal more traffic. How can you reconcile your two positions?

You might explain:

> The character of the neighborhood has changed dramatically over the past five years. Despite my protests, the zoning board repeatedly allowed high-density uses along the streets bordering Elmwood Forest. As a result, property values plummeted. The neighborhood is no longer inhabited by upwardly mobile young people, but largely by the elderly and the poor. These people need the services this office would provide.

5. *Hypothetical questions.* Avoid responding to speculation. Base your answers on what you know to be fact. Your interviewer says:

> You've said that you need a 10,000-square-foot building and no more than twenty parking spaces for the office you have in mind. Suppose the city limits you to 8,000 square feet and requires you to provide thirty parking spaces. What would you do?

Your response might be:

> I can respond only to what we know at this time. Current plans call for a 10,000-square-foot building with up to twenty parking spaces.

6. *Loaded prefaces.* When the interviewer's preface contains confrontational, highly charged, negative language, make sure you take the sting out of the question before answering. The interviewer says:

> Last year your organization spearheaded the establishment of the John F. Kennedy Municipal Park in a low-income neighborhood. To clear land for the park, the city tore down thirty homes. Now you're proposing the new Martin Luther King Park in another low-income neighborhood. How many people will this park put out into the streets?

This is analogous to the "Have you stopped beating your wife?" question. If you answer the question directly, you are accepting the loaded proposition. Your answer might be:

> We maintain a proactive program to meet our community's housing needs. We eliminated thirty substandard dwellings when we established John F. Kennedy Park. Of these, eighteen were abandoned and vacant. The families occupying the remaining twelve were relocated in safe, sanitary public housing. We expect to raze a comparable number of substandard dwellings when we establish Martin Luther King Park, and will follow the same procedure in relocating families. This way, the parks project will accomplish two objectives. It will provide recreational facilities for residents of a low-income area. It will also move families out of unsafe, unsanitary dwellings into more wholesome surroundings.

7. *Nonquestions.* Sometimes, an interviewer will give a lengthy preamble and never ask a question. When this happens, respond with questions for more details, then amplify or refute the reporter's information. The interviewer may say something like this:

> This city already has more park space per capita than the National League of Cities recommends, while its inventory of decent housing is dwindling. There's a long waiting list for public housing, while the public park in Casa Royale is under-utilized. . . .

You might respond with questions such as these:

• Are you asking whether we should build parks in low-income areas while parks in high-income areas such as Casa Royale are under-utilized?

• Are you asking whether we should stop building parks until the waiting list for public housing has disappeared?

• Are you asking whether we should allow substandard housing to stand in the way of a public park because we don't have enough decent housing?

Then you could go to the refutation:

> The ratio of park acreage to people is certainly high in the city as a whole. Unfortunately, it's well below national standards in the eastern half of the city. This area happens to be the low-income section. Since the completion of John F. Kennedy Park, the incidence of juvenile crime in the immediate area has dropped by 10 percent. The kids now have something else to do besides hang out at crack houses.

8. *Questions containing unfamiliar information.* When the questioner throws unfamiliar information at you, do not respond as though the facts were accurate. Say that you are unfamiliar with the information or its source, and, therefore, you cannot comment on it. If the interviewer persists, say, "If you will provide me with the source of your information, I will be glad to examine it and get back with you later."

9. *False facts (unintentional or deliberate).* When the interviewer tosses out inaccurate information—

whether deliberately or unintentionally—correct the mistake graciously, then make a positive point. The interviewer says:

> The new convention center you're advocating will require a 10-percent increase in property taxes and will require a major bond issue. How can you justify this kind of spending during an economic downturn?

You might reply:

> Let me clarify that for you, Steve. The tax increase to which you refer has nothing to do with the convention center. The city's tax base has declined, and the tax increase is necessary to keep revenues level, even without further expenditures. The convention center will not be built with general-obligation bonds issued by the city, and will not be paid for with tax funds. We're proposing that the Industrial Authority issue revenue bonds, to be repaid with revenue from the center. In these economic doldrums, the convention center makes eminently good sense. It will bring in new money in the form of conventions and trade shows. It will enhance the city's attractiveness as a location for new business. And it will increase the value of surrounding properties, resulting in more property-tax revenue for the city.

10. *Questions involving a reinterpretation of your response.* You have just told your interviewer that,

although sales in apparel fabrics are going well, the sheeting and piece goods market has fallen off considerably, necessitating a production cutback. Your interviewer responds:

> So we're looking at some possible plant closures.

In your response, do not repeat the loaded words. Pause, then say:

> These particular segments of our business were not up to our expectations during the first quarter. We've temporarily curtailed production at these plants while we analyze the market for more profitable lines that we might produce there.

11. *Questions based on false assumptions or conclusions.* Your interviewer says:

> So if you can't find another line of products that you can produce profitably in those plants, you'll have to close them down.

Your response should be to call this technique what it is:

> That's an assumption. Let's consider the facts. The textile business, like most other businesses, is cyclical. Even if we conclude that it would be unprofitable to convert to another type of fabric, we expect the sheeting and piece goods markets to pick up by the end of the next

quarter so that we can resume normal
production.

12. *Questions that put words in your mouth.* Your
interviewer comments:

> So you're saying that you've been laying
> off workers unnecessarily since the mar-
> ket for their products is bound to pick up
> during the next quarter.

In your response, do not say, "No, we have not been
laying workers off unnecessarily. . . ." Remember that
to repeat the offending words is to add credence to
them through verbal reinforcement—even when you
repeat them as part of the denial. Do not argue
with the interviewer. Your response might follow
this line:

> Let's see what's at issue here, Tom. We're
> experiencing a period of market adjust-
> ment. During this time, we must decide
> whether the present product lines offer
> the most long-term profitability. It
> wouldn't make sense for us to continue
> full production of the products while
> demand is soft and there are no ready
> buyers. When the market gets stronger,
> we plan to respond aggressively. That
> means that long-term employment pros-
> pects look good once we get past this
> temporary downturn.

13. *Questions based on false statistics or faulty logic.*
When you have a question that hinges upon a statistic
or an argument you know is wrong, remain courteous

but question it. Ask for the source. Ask for the opportunity to see the document. Remain helpful and cooperative. You may know the statement is not true, but you do not have the correct information at hand to refute it. If this is the case, politely say that you do not believe that the information is correct. Leave yourself a way out so that you can graciously offer to get back with a clarification or correction.

14. *Multiple questions.* Sometimes interviewers turn all the questions going through their minds into lengthy, run-on questions. When this happens, it is all right *not* to be 100 percent responsive. You might pick out the one question that you most want to answer and answer it. Or you might say, "You've asked me several questions. The issue that covers them all is. . . ." If you are in a situation in which you need more time to think about your response, ask for a restatement of one question or more, or a confirmation of specific items the interviewer has asked for. If you elect to answer several questions, take the most difficult one first. This allows you to move on to more comfortable questions and end on a positive note.

15. *Needling questions.* The interviewer may feign incredulity and say, "Oh, come now. Do you really expect us to believe that?" When that happens, stick to your guns. Do not equivocate or vacillate, and do not be defensive. Say, "Yes, Fran, that's what the facts indicate." Then go on to reinforce the positive point just made, or to make a new positive point.

"No Comment" and "I Don't Know"

The two words to avoid during interviews are "No comment." These words sound hostile and create the impression that you are trying to cover something up. If you cannot answer the question because you do not know the answer, say, "I don't know." Then, give action and a timetable for that action. And deliver the information you say you will deliver when you said you would deliver it. If you cannot answer for other reasons, say that you are unable to answer and explain why:

> I'm unable to answer that question because it deals with sensitive and private personnel matters.

Remember Your Objective

Always remember the purpose of your interview: to win the audience over to your conclusion. Aim for a power presentation, using high-impact words to convey your thoughts. Words such as *advantage, deserve, easy, guarantee, health, love, modern, money, positive, quality, safety, success, value,* and *you* add power and credibility to your speech.

Try to create a memorable impression with your audience. Somewhere during the interview, look for the opportunity to seize the "perfect moment." Maintain an interesting delivery that will hold your audience's attention. Incorporate an entertaining style that lets your personality, humanity, and energy show through. Your presentation should display optimism and enthusiasm, as well as an ability to laugh at yourself. Be ethical at all costs, and be credible.

And remember: this is *your* interview. Use it to make your point, to communicate *your* message.

In Summary:

- Your objective during an interview should be to communicate the message *you* want to convey.

- Suggest a site appropriate to the topic.

- Thoroughly familiarize yourself with the material to be covered in the interview.

- Familiarize yourself with the program; learn what interviewees are expected to provide.

- Try to anticipate the questions you will be asked and rehearse your answers.

- Prepare "focus statements," which summarize key points you want to make in eighty words or less.

- At the interview site, build rapport with the interviewer through pleasant conversation prior to the interview.

- Use the minutes leading up to the interview to organize your thoughts into small, workable chunks.

- If you experience nervousness, learn some relaxation techniques and put them into practice.

- Learn to deal with:
  1. Questions you *can* answer and *want* to answer.
  2. Questions you *can* answer, but would *rather not* answer directly.
  3. Questions you *cannot* answer.

- Review the different types of difficult questions and practice dealing with them.

- Aim for a power presentation. Be positive, be truthful, be ethical, be entertaining, be enthusiastic, and be in control.

9

Putting Power into Public Presentations

The person who expects to lead must be able to inform, inspire, and persuade others. This calls for power communications.

Media mastery is an important way of communicating with power, but it is not enough. Before you can persuade and inspire a mass audience, you must be able to persuade and inspire those around you. Before you can communicate with power through television, radio, or newspaper, you must be able to communicate with power in person.

This means that you must be prepared to face live audiences and share with them your ideas and visions. You must be able to take their questions and answer them honestly and convincingly. In short, to succeed, public persons need to express themselves effectively as public speakers.

Recognize that, when addressing a live audience or

your ultimate media audience, you must focus on two levels of need. You go into the program or interview knowing the message you need to convey to get your point across. Unfortunately, this is where most speakers stop. To make a connection with your message, however, you also must convey information based on the perceived need or needs of your audience. Without connecting the two levels of need, your audience is often left wanting. No matter what a listener's particular focus, people have six basic needs that you will want to satisfy. The effective communicator will address as many of these as possible to fortify the connection with an audience. These needs are to feel secure, to belong, to be presented with opportunity, to advance in their fields or communities, to be recognized, and to make a contribution to society.

These needs, coupled with the basic motivations of *pain* and/or *gain,* will help you, as a speaker or public person in other environments, to develop the link between you, your message, and the receiver of that information. Let me give you an example of why you want to be aware of the pain-and/or-gain influence on your message. Traditionally, the insurance industry has succeeded because it appeals to the public's basic fears of being caught without financial protection. They have sold policies based on fear; this fear is perceived pain. In the past several years, insurance agents have been able to expand their services to include financial planning and investments. This gives agents the opportunity to help their clients invest and grow their money. This is a perceived gain. Therefore, the insurance industry can now sell its products based on the motivations of pain and gain. You will find that many businesses, like the insurance industry, and most situations can be perceived in terms of pain and gain.

Occasions for Public Presentations

Public presentations are demanded in many different situations. As an executive or manager, you will often appear before groups of employees to explain company policy. Maybe you will need to persuade them to buy into the corporate vision. You might need to convince them of the necessity of taking certain actions or accepting certain sacrifices to achieve corporate goals. Or you could be called upon to give public recognition to those who have made exemplary contributions.

Sometimes you will be asked to make presentations to potential clients. You might find yourself going before governmental boards and commissions to ask for zoning changes, exemptions from regulations, or special permits to allow you to do business. Officials could ask you to appear during public meetings to explain controversial policies to the public.

Your community relations activities will provide you with many opportunities to obtain positive visibility through speeches to civic clubs, school audiences, and other forums. Many people recoil at the idea of facing live audiences. In fact, the fear of public speaking is said to be the most widespread phobia in America. With the proper preparation, however, you can mount the platform with confidence and turn public speaking into a powerful tool for success.

Do Your Homework

The preparation for your public presentation begins before you agree to speak. Learn as much as you can about the background and history of the organization that extends the invitation. Get precise details about the speaking arrangements: date, time, place, subject, agenda, length of speech, question-and-answer opportunities, special needs, and interests of the group.

Find out whether there will be other speakers. Who are they? What are their topics? In what order will they speak? How should your speech relate to their speeches and to the entire program?

Your position on the program will determine the nature and tone of your presentation. If you are the first speaker in the morning, you will want to be lively and fresh in your presentation, though you do not want to be too exuberant or you could overwhelm your audience. If you are speaking at the end of a long session, you will want to be upbeat and energizing. If you are the last speaker of the day, or if you follow a boring speaker, you will want to be entertaining.

Find out what the group will be doing immediately before and after your presentation. Relating your introduction and conclusion to these activities will help you establish rapport. Find out about the format. Will it be a panel discussion or an individual presentation? Will a question-and-answer session follow your speech, or occur at the end of the program?

What size audience will you be facing? What type of people will be attending? What are the business, professional, or personal interests of the group? How much will they already know about your topic? What will they want to learn from you? Will the audience be all men, all women, or mixed? What age group will predominate? Are there any cultural idiosyncrasies? What does the audience expect to take away from the session? Is your audience there by choice or mandate? What other speakers have addressed the group on similar, related, or opposing issues?

What will be the room arrangements? Will there be a podium or lectern? Will there be a microphone? If so, what kind? What kind of seating arrangement can you expect? Will there be provisions for visual aids? Will it be permissible to provide handouts or other materials? Who will introduce you? Will that person need a personal biography, a written introduction, or a personal anecdote about you?

Once you have all this information in hand, you can decide whether the occasion will offer you an opportunity to make a positive statement about yourself, your organization, and your ideas. Is the group hostile to your objectives? Then you must decide whether there is a possibility of persuading it or at least softening the opposition. Obviously, you do not want to walk into a figurative lynching party; however, do not overlook opportunities to win people to your side.

Consider, too, whether your words might reach a larger audience. If the media are covering the event, and you communicate with power, your words may reach far beyond the walls of the meeting hall. Even if you do not persuade your direct audience, you can make a positive impression on those in the media audience. In addition to the media's coverage of the event itself, you might be interviewed before or after the presentation. This can create an opportunity for you to refine the message you convey.

Once you have accepted the invitation, it is time to work on your speech. Prepare a work sheet to guide you in constructing an effective power presentation. Start with the topic. What, essentially, are you going to talk about, and how much time will you have to cover your subject? Next, write down the key points you want to make. These will serve as the skeleton for your speech.

Write down any stories, anecdotes, or quotes that might add color to your presentation. Decide on the purpose or multiple purposes of your speech. Is it to inform, to educate, to entertain, to persuade, to inspire, or to activate your audience? What other objectives might it serve?

Note the details of the audience. This will help you to decide which points will have the greatest impact on the people you are addressing and what stories and anecdotes will capture their attention.

Decide how you want to open and close your speech. You might begin with questions that you expect to answer during your speech. You might begin and end with humor. A good story, especially a personal one, often makes a good introduction. And a closing illustration can be effective in driving home your point. You can also use quotations, statistics, and comparisons to begin or conclude your presentation.

You will also want to prepare for questions and answers that will follow your speech. To get ready for these, review the points covered in the preceding chapter. Preparing for audience questions parallels your preparation for an interviewer's questions. In essence, you are being interviewed by the audience. You will also want to work out a schedule for speech rehearsals and question-and-answer practice.

If you are going to wow your audience, you must do more than *know* your subject; you will have to *master* it. The first step toward this mastery requires you to decide what you want to accomplish, both generally and specifically. Your general objective may be to convince your audience that the plant your company plans to build in the community will be a good neighbor and an asset to the area. Your specific objective may be to persuade responsible authorities to approve the necessary zonings and permits.

Your objectives will guide you in your research. Your research begins where your present knowledge ends. How much do you know already? What special knowledge have you acquired that sets you apart from others who might approach this subject? What unusual personal experiences have you had that might lend you credibility? How much will you need to learn about the topic to be able to give an authoritative presentation and handle an audience question-and-answer session?

Then look for the facts, statistics, and actual examples to support your ideas. Draw upon your imagination for hypothetical examples and on your experiences for personal examples. The most effective research is firsthand and original. You can find lots of material on the former Soviet Union in encyclopedias, atlases, books, and periodicals. But if you have actually *been* there, and witnessed Communism at work in Soviet society, you gain immensely more credibility.

The same is true of other topics. On-site observations, firsthand interviews, and personal impressions can add authority to your presentation. This does not mean that you should not go near the library. On few topics will your firsthand knowledge match the accumulated lore to be found on library shelves. If there is a specialized library with materials on your topic, make use of it. These materials can provide solid confirmation for your own observations.

Look for quotes from recognized authorities to illustrate or illuminate the points you make. Look for episodes in current events to add color and relevance to your presentation. The news, sports, features, and entertainment columns of newspapers and periodicals can be rich sources of material.

Writing the Speech

When you think you have thoroughly mastered the subject and have accumulated all the information you need, it is time to proceed with the actual speech writing.

Writing is essentially a process of organizing ideas and information. Your purpose is to organize the mass of material you have accumulated into an orderly, coherent, stimulating presentation that your audience can easily understand and act upon in some way.

In the age of television, the attention span of the American audience has shrunk considerably. Speakers who expound for longer than a half-hour are likely to lose substantial portions of their audiences. Even a twenty-minute presentation must be broken down into short, easily digestible "chunks" of information if you want to maintain the audience's attention.

Before you actually write your speech, sit down and

let your mind wander over your material and your audience. Write down your thoughts and ideas as they come to mind. Do not worry about the order in which they come. You are engaged in one-person brainstorming at this point, and the object is to get as many ideas as possible on paper.

Once you have all your ideas on paper, analyze them to see what they have in common. Group them into clusters of related ideas. The ideas within a cluster may not fit as smoothly as the pieces of a jigsaw puzzle. But if an idea bears *some* relationship to other ideas in a cluster, go ahead and include it.

For maximum effectiveness, your speech should have no more than five clusters; three is even better. You want to arrange the clusters in the most effective order. Begin the process by picking the cluster that will come last in your speech. You do this to discern the conclusive message you want to leave with your audience. Be sure to organize your ideas and information logically and understandably.

Then choose the cluster that will precede it. This should be the information that connects with the final cluster. The last cluster you fit into place should be the one that will come first in your speech. This segment functions as an introduction for your entire presentation, as well as a bridge to more in-depth treatment of the information you want to share. The introduction also is where you need to establish a relationship with your audience.

Once you have identified your beginning, middle, and closing clusters, flesh them out by entering all the information you plan to use in the appropriate clusters.

Fine-Tune Your Conclusion First

When you develop your closing, remember to choose words carefully so that you can use them concisely and dramatically to express ideas. Be brief and know your conclusion; do not read it. Following are several techniques you can use to close your presentation:

- **Summarize what you have said.** Concisely reinforce the central message of your speech; do not merely repeat what you have said.

- **Link your conclusion to your introduction.** This helps you complete the delivery of information you will be introducing at the beginning of your presentation.

- **Detail a plan.** Describe precise step-by-step actions the listeners can take and motivate them to effect that plan.

- **Challenge your audience.** Encourage it to change or enhance its attitudes and actions, especially as they relate to the material you have presented. As a natural extension of this, you can provide alternatives for them to adopt.

- **Use an interest-generating technique.** Ask a question, use a quotation, tell a story, or read a poem. Remember: whichever technique you use must be relevant to what you have been addressing.

- **Congratulate your listeners.** Thank them for their involvement in and contribution to your program. This provides one last opportunity for rapport with your audience and can leave them with a positive impression of you and your message.

- **Make yourself available for follow-up.** This technique also maintains an open door between you and your audience and invites future interaction between you and your listeners.

- **Demonstrate the meaning and value of your message to your audience.** This answers the six basic needs we discussed earlier in this chapter that your listeners want you to meet.

Next Comes the Middle . . . Then the Beginning

When you develop the internal part of your speech, also called the body, you want to remember that this segment contains the substance of your presentation. Here are several ways for you to present your internal material:

- **Topical.** List facts point by point, subject by subject, as part of a whole concept.

- **Spatial.** Emphasize the physical order or sequence in which things happen, helping the listener to follow along.

- **Problem/Solution.** Tell the listeners what is wrong and how they can fix it.

- **Chronological.** Organize your facts in time sequence.

- **Logical.** Explain the reasons behind what you are saying.[1]

- **"What if ... ?"** Create interactive opportunities for your audience to personally relate to your information by posing hypothetical questions or scenarios for them to answer collectively or individually, out loud or mentally.

After you have drafted the middle of your speech, you can decide which type of beginning you will use. It is important for you to think of your introduction not in terms of what will open up the audience but rather in terms of what will invite the audience to listen. You will want to begin with impact to create an immediate interest. Remember that, ordinarily, you have only about sixty seconds to develop a relationship with your audience.

The most successful openers need to be relevant to the audience, appropriate to the setting, and effectively suit your own personal style. You can choose from the following approaches to begin your presentation:

- **Describe the subject area in general terms.** If your speech is about a particular bill in Congress, you can give an overview of the legislative process. If it is about Keynesian theory, you might give a brief description of how economics works in a free-market society.

- **Focus on a specific element of the subject.** If you are talking about air pollution, you might start with acid rain and move on to the factors that affect overall air quality, including the greenhouse effect.

- **Create a better understanding for your audience.** If your subject is unfamiliar to your audience, draw an analogy with something the audience knows. If, for example, you are discussing budgetary and staff cut-backs at the corporate level, you could explain this in terms of the effect on a family budget when one of the wage-earners loses a job.

- **Lay a foundation for your theme.** If you are advocating the continuation of a nonprofit trust fund, you might preface your remarks with a background on the fund and why it is important to the community.

- **Explain why you are addressing this audience with this message.** For example, you might cite a newspaper headline that relates to your audience and explain how your message will directly impact the headline and the audience.

- **Get their attention.** Just as with the conclusion, you can use quotations, questions, stories, personal anecdotes, and personal humor to introduce your presentation. Again, recognize that these approaches must be relevant and used in good taste.

Putting Power into Your Speech Writing

Now that you have organized your material, your task is to express it in a clear and forceful way. Remember that the purpose of a speech is to *communicate,* not to show off your vocabulary. Your intention should be to express ideas, not to impress people. Use simple words and simple, forceful sentences. Big words and long sentences do not equate with eloquence. More than three-fourths of the words Abraham Lincoln used in the Gettysburg Address were of five letters or less.

Your audience has trouble following long sentences, and they are hard for you to deliver. Read your sentences aloud. Any sentence that is so long that it requires you to stop for breath is too long. Recast the long sentence into two or more short, speakable ones. When you do use a long sentence, follow it with a short one to give the listener's mind a break. This will give rhythm and variety to your speech. Notice how Lincoln alternated long and short sentences in his Gettysburg Address:

> Now we are engaged in a great civil war, testing whether that nation or any nation so conceived and so dedicated can long endure. (25 words.) We are met on a great battlefield of that war. (10 words.) We have come to dedicate a portion of that field, as a final resting place for those who here gave their lives that that nation might live. (27 words.) It is altogether fitting and proper that we should do this. (11 words.)

Write for the ear, not for the eye. Choose words that you can pronounce easily and smoothly. Avoid tongue-twisters. Never be content with the first draft of your speech. Read it aloud to make sure that it flows easily from your lips. Weed out words that do not fit or that slow down the delivery and impede comprehension.

Add color to your speech through the use of anecdotes, analogies, similes, and metaphors. These illustrations enable the speaker to convey ideas in terms the listener can more readily understand.

Anecdotes can be real or fictitious stories that illustrate a point you are making. Several years ago I met Mike Wallace prior to a *60 Minutes* interview. While his production crew was setting up I worked with his guest to help him prepare for the interview. I asked Wallace if we could audiotape the interview while his crew filmed it. He gave me the go-ahead to tape, with a restriction that I could only tape during filming. He said he had once given the same permission to another person who taped when the cameras were not rolling. That recording inadvertently included conversational remarks Wallace did not want to be made public. However, because of Wallace's public profile, the recording was susceptible to the very public exposure he wanted to avoid. This anecdote reinforces the principle that public persons are always accountable for their words and actions.

Analogies enable you to compare the unfamiliar to the familiar. A newspaper writer, once trying to explain how a nuclear reaction was started in a nuclear power plant, compared the uranium atom with a rack of balls on a pool table. The "balls"—the neutrons, protons, and electrons that made up the atom—were waiting only for a "cue ball," a stray neutron, to strike them, thus starting a chain reaction similar to what happens on the break. The analogy made it easier for anyone who had played pool or witnessed a pool game to visualize what happens in a nuclear reaction.

Similes and *metaphors* are colorful ways of expressing analogies. The word "like" is the identifying feature of a simile. "Like a cat on a hot tin roof" is a familiar simile. Look for opportunities to compare the unfamiliar to the familiar through similes and metaphors.

The head of a regional sanitation commission once described what happened when an excessive load of pollutants was released into a treatment plant. The plant used a mass of bacteria—a bio-mass—to break down the pollutants. When the load became excessive the undigested pollutants would build up to a certain point. Then the plant would emit a metaphorical "burp," discharging the pollution over a weir and into the river. The "burp" was an apt metaphor for the technical process.

You can use metaphors and similes to paint vivid pictures in your listener's mind. Look for ways to bring sights, sounds, and smells to life. A newspaper columnist used these devices in describing a drought-breaking rain in his area:

> It was not a memorable rain, the one that soothed our valley last week with its slow, patient downpour, washing the film of pollution off the face of the mountains. But it was a timely torrent, slaking the area's thirst like a lingering draught from a gourd dipper, filled from a sheltered spring, after a hard day in the fields.

"Washing the film of pollution off the face of the mountains" is a metaphor. "Like a lingering draught from a gourd dipper" is a simile.

Draw these illustrations from your own wealth of experience, keeping in mind the nature of your audience. Your metaphors, similes, and analogies should use comparisons that will be familiar to your audience.

Don't Use Strange Abbreviations

Speakers and writers often like to use abbreviations and acronyms to demonstrate their familiarity with a subject. This can force the reader or listener to swim through a sea of alphabet soup.

Some abbreviations are more readily understood than the full expressions they stand for. FBI, CIA, IRS, and PLO are examples. Some organizations are known almost exclusively by their acronyms, such as NATO and NASA.

Still, in most cases it is best for you to explain the abbreviations you use—at least on first reference. AAA can stand for Amateur Athletic Association as well as American Automobile Association. An AG can be an adjutant general as well as an attorney general. Not everyone knows that OSHA stands for Occupational Safety and Health Administration, much less that IHP stands for indicated horsepower.

Avoid foreign expressions that are not part of everyday language. Unless you are speaking to a group of Francophiles, you should delete such expressions as *de rigueur* and *de trop*. If you find that you *must* use a foreign expression, be sure you know the correct pronunciation.

Practice, Practice, Practice

After you have written your speech, the next step is to practice, practice, practice. Practice before a mirror and into a tape recorder, or, better yet, into a video camera. Speak and act just as you plan to do when you are actually delivering your speech.

Play back the tape and make note of the places where you sped up, slowed down, stressed a word, and increased or lowered your volume. Make notes in your text of the places where such techniques are effective. As you practice again, follow these notations. Replay the tape over and over until you have delivered the presentation just the way you want it. Seeing yourself successfully deliver your speech on video tape will enhance your visualization of a successful presentation before your audience.

On the Platform

You are sitting on the platform now, or at the banquet table, ready to be introduced. The chairperson has gone through a brief biography, given the topic of your speech, and introduced you by name. You're on!

Approach the lectern with calm, confident stride. There is no need to run, skip, or jump, unless that is part of some entertainment routine. Nor should you walk slowly and hesitantly, as if you are not sure whether it is your turn to speak. Take a moment to smile and establish eye contact with your audience, then begin your speech.

The safest posture to assume during a presentation

is the authority posture. Stand straight, but not ramrod straight. Keep your shoulders back and maintain an attitude of relaxed alertness. Keep your feet flat on the floor, slightly apart, and keep your weight balanced between them. Do not shift your weight from one foot to the other. Place your hands on the sides of the lectern at the rear. Do not grip the lectern; just let your hands rest there until you are ready to gesture. If there is no lectern, maintain the same posture. Use the hand position that comes most naturally to you. A visually acceptable one is to let your hands rest at your sides.

For less formal interactions, you might prefer the casual posture. Because you are more relaxed in this mode, you may sit on the edge of a table or lean against the lectern. You might come out from behind the lectern and walk around a bit or not even use a lectern. Your hands will be more mobile, and you can even put them in your pocket at times.

The authority posture is more common at news conferences and other formal stand-up speaking events. It helps to convey an image of strength and helps neutralize intimidating or hostile audiences. If you are a young middle manager and you are asked to give a presentation to the full board, or if you are an elected official appearing before constituents who have recently been made homeless by a devastating hurricane, use the authority posture. If you are the leader of an educational workshop, an employer trying to relax a group of subordinates, or an impromptu speaker in an informal setting, use the informal posture.

From the outset, establish eye contact with your audience. This provides two-way communication between you and your listeners. Look into the eyes of individuals. Do not look at the back of the room, or let your eyes scan unfocused over the entire audience.

Look for individuals who look back at you with expressions of interest, friendliness, and agreement. They will provide you with welcome moral support during your presentation. Look at each individual long enough to create a visual mutual understanding, then move on to someone else. Let your own expression reflect friendliness and sincerity.

Here is one technique you can use if the audience is large: mentally divide your listeners into groups of five to ten people. Let your eyes move from one group to another, making eye contact with one person in each group with each tour of the room.

If you use visual aids, make sure they are relevant to your subject, that they are visible and understandable, and that they are listener-oriented. Do not work with visual aids unless you have practiced with them and feel confident in your ability to work with them and the information they contain.

Even when you are using the overhead projector, the flip chart or the slide projector, do not lose eye contact with your listeners. Talk to the audience, not to the visual aids or the items you are demonstrating, but be aware of what your audience is seeing. One speaker was well into his slide presentation before he realized that he had brought the wrong tray of slides.

Do not show everything at once. Focus attention on one point, one step, and one object at a time. Visual aids should enhance the speaker's performance; they cannot replace it. Remember, the most important factor in informing and persuading the audience is you, the power presenter, not the visuals.

On most occasions, you will face friendly audiences. Sometimes, though, you will focus your presentation on defusing anger or neutralizing opposition. On such occasions, preface your particular pivotal point with defusers. Acknowledge, with appreciation, that some members of the audience may not share your views. Be as positive as you can when you make this statement. Then, thank them for taking the time to listen and for giving you the opportunity to share your views with them. Follow this, in your presentation, by building as many common bonds as you can, while minimizing the differences in your perspectives.

Taking Questions

Many speakers like to conclude their presentations by taking questions from the audience. Preparation for these sessions parallels the preparation for media interviews described in chapter 8. Anticipate the questions you are likely to be asked. Prepare focus statements that cover the points you want to make, and be prepared to re-direct to these statements.

Usually, the speaker chooses the questioners from the audience. If it is up to you, take questions from all parts of the audience—not just those up front. Listen carefully to each question. Do not smile and do not frown as the question is posed. Show interest and attention and let your face respond, with your body and words, when it is time for you to answer.

Treat every questioner equally. If you say "good question" to one questioner, you are implying that other questions are not so good. Repeat all positive questions and paraphrase the negative ones. This lets you set the tone and emphasis for your answer.

As you answer, look first at the person who asked the question. Then let your eye contact take in the whole audience. You can apply the 25–75 rule: 25 percent of your total visual contact time with the questioner and 75 percent with the rest of the audience.

Respond simply and directly. Do not extend your answers because the more you say, the greater the chance that you will go too far. On the other hand, be careful about limiting yourself by saying, "This will be our last question." You may want to try for one more positive question so that you can leave your audience with a strong response.

What if the audience does not have a question? Try priming the pump. Say, "Last week, when I spoke to the National Leadership Association, members asked me about. . . . " If someone asks a question you have already answered in your speech, answer it again. Incorporate another approach to fortify the information. If someone asks a question that has already been asked, do not answer it twice. Say, "We've already talked about that. However, I'll be happy to talk with you about it in more detail after our program."

If someone tries to turn a question into a long-winded speech, interrupt politely but firmly "in the interest of saving time." Irrelevant questions can be handled with a simple, "I'll be happy to talk about that subject with you later. (Pause) The subject we're discussing right now involves employee benefits."

Sometimes a question is so disorganized it defies a coherent answer. You can respond to just one part and ignore the rest. Pick the part that you know best and one that will help reinforce your message.

If you do not know the answer to a question, do not fake it. Say you do not know, and offer to get the information to the person, or offer to prepare a response and mail it to your audience's president, if appropriate.

You can put credibility into your answers in a number of ways. Here are some of them:

1. Cite your own professional experience.

2. Refer to your own personal experience.

3. Quote experts.

4. Present facts.

5. Disassociate, with a response such as, "That was the policy during the last administration. Our policy is. . . ."

6. Establish a bond. Say, "I can certainly appreciate your concern."

7. Recognize the importance of the question, but be careful not to sound patronizing. Also, be careful not to "single out" questions.

8. Use one-liners, prepared ahead of time, that will stick in the minds of the audience and that the media can quote.

You will encounter a number of different types of questioners in any given audience. Some will be friendly, some hostile, some just annoying. Look for these types:

• **The Advocate.** This questioner offers supportive comments about you and your statements. Appreciate this person. Convey open and sincere thanks for the kind words and tell the audience why you are gratified. Add a selling point, a further example of achievements you believe are praiseworthy: "Thanks very much, Mr. Wilson. We appreciate your involvement in this program. It is nice to know that you appreciate our efforts. A recent addition to that program is. . . ."

- **The Nitpicker.** This person likes to quibble over facts and figures. Your natural response to this provocation would be to enter a debate, but don't. Often, the nitpicker's point is minor and insignificant. Politeness requires that you spend time with the questioner. However, if you spend too much time, you lose everybody else. So deal with the question as quickly as possible. If you are aware of your facts and figures, stand by them. If there is legitimate room for disagreement, volunteer to see the person after this exchange to resolve the matter. Say, "Why don't we discuss this after we finish here? I'll look at your information and get back to you by Friday." Then follow up on your commitment.

- **The Rambler.** This nonquestioner launches into an aimless, run-on statement which, though you might anticipate a question, never gets to that point. Actually, the questioner is merely thinking out loud and the statement is almost always negative or critical in tone. Rarely does it contain an explicit point you can come to grips with and address. It tends to make you and the others present uncomfortable, and the source of discomfort is your loss of control. You have nothing to respond to; the questioner has taken the steering wheel. You cannot politely interrupt with, "Are you going to ask a question?" However, if the rambler gives you an opening, you can jump in and regain control by "answering," "Well, Ms. Thompson, if I understand what you're asking. . . ." When the speaker gives you no opening, you have only one recourse—to use the baton-passing technique. Listen politely until you hear a key word or phrase, reach out, grab the word—and the monologue—and run with it. For instance, if the rambler mentions the word "economy," you might jump in quickly: "I'm glad you brought up the economy. Did you know that this state spent $10 million on its economic recruitment efforts last year? And, even with this reduced spending, our state gained twice as many relocated businesses as the year before."

- **The Nay-Sayer.** This questioner has a personal problem or a negative statement. It is clearly not a question at all, so when this person confronts you, respond; do not get sidetracked. Take the problem where it belongs—outside the bounds of the present meeting or presentation. Respond, if possible, to the issue being raised, even if it is only to validate or acknowledge it. Show your willingness to help and the restrictions you are operating under in this situation. Then, make yourself available to that person for additional dialogue.

- **The Rover.** Rather than focusing on a particular idea or subject, this person meanders all over the stadium. When you encounter the rover, take control and focus the subject and question yourself. Suggest a specific question: "Are you asking me whether I favor abolishing the program or replacing the president?" Then proceed to answer the question you have offered.

The Last-Minute Invitation

Sometimes the invitation to speak comes at the last minute, giving you little or no time to rehearse or carefully plan your presentation. Perhaps it is a sales presentation to an important customer, a proposal to the board of directors, an appearance before a regulatory board, or a substitute speech for a scheduled speaker who came down with laryngitis.

You can be ready for such occasions, if you prepare in advance. Keep a generic speech in your files. The presentation should deal with your field of expertise. Update it from time to time. Let this speech serve as the core of your impromptu presentation. You can vary your introduction, illustrations, and details of content, according to the group you are addressing.

Keep a file of all the visual props you have used at past presentations. Mary Duhon, director of communications for Airco, an American subsidiary of the British BOC Group, says she photographs or videotapes everything new—ads, sales brochures, customer applications, or trade-show displays—and keeps them on file for future presentations. She can augment them with overheads that cover last-minute information or tailor the data to the audience.

Get on the distribution list for all reports and publications pertinent to your area of responsibility, and keep them on file. These current materials can provide valuable quick sources of information for last-minute speeches. Also, develop a formula for tailoring your material to the group you are addressing. You will want to ask yourself the following questions:

• What does my audience already know about my subject?

- What does the audience need to know, based on both my perceptions and those of the audience?

- How can I make the information I plan to share easy to understand and use?

- How can I best attract and keep their interest throughout this presentation?

- What main thought or thoughts do I want the audience to understand by the time I have finished my presentation?

- What can I do to motivate the listeners to act on my ideas or suggestions after they leave this room?

With proper preparation, you can be ready to mount the speaker's platform on a moment's notice. When your community learns that you have that capability, you will see a rise in demand for you as a public speaker. Your community will recognize you as a powerful communicator and a community asset. In short, you will demonstrate your skills as an articulate public person.

In Summary:

- People seeking public personhood must be willing and able to make public presentations, whether speeches before civic groups, presentations to customers, speeches to employees, or appearances before regulatory bodies.

- Before you agree to speak, learn as much as you can about the background and history of the organization that extends the invitation, the topic it wants you to speak about, the nature of the program, and the order in which you will appear.

- Find out what role you might have in promoting the speech. Look for opportunities to build up an audience.

- Prepare thoroughly for the speech; master the subject.

- Organize your speech into clusters of related information and place these clusters in the reverse order in which you will cover them: the conclusion, the middle, and the introduction.

- Write your speech for the ear instead of for the eye. Use short, simple words and short sentences. Deliver your presentation as a dialogue, not as a reading.

- Rehearse your presentation before a mirror, on audiotape, or, better yet, on videotape.

- At the lectern, you may assume one of two basic postures:

  1. The authority posture, for news conferences and other formal stand-up occasions in which you need to project authority.
  2. The casual posture, for less formal occasions when you want to establish an atmosphere of friendliness and intimacy.

- Follow these tips for delivery of your presentation:

  1. Maintain eye contact with people throughout the audience.

2. Let your voice, body, and words convey conviction.

3. Use appropriate gestures to punctuate your speech.

4. If you use visual aids, make them relevant to your subject. Talk to your audience, not to your visuals.

- When facing a hostile audience or one you know does not share your viewpoint, acknowledge your differences and build common bonds.

- If you plan to take questions from the audience, prepare for them in advance by anticipating the questions you will receive and by preparing focus statements to which you can bridge.

- Recognize and know how to handle the types of questioners you may encounter: advocates, ramblers, nitpickers, nay-sayers, and rovers.

- Have a generic speech on hand at all times to serve as core material in the event you are asked to give a last-minute presentation. Keep files for articles and visual aids, and update them regularly.

- Develop a formula for adapting your material to individual audiences.

Notes

1. Stephen C. Rafe, *How to Be Prepared to Think on Your Feet* (New York: Harper Business, 1990), 79.

10

Confronting a Crisis

public person is a leader, and a leader is never far from the center of action. When you find yourself at the center of action, all eyes are on you. They see you in your moments of glory and during your pratfalls. They see you when you are riding the swell of success and when you are up to your waist in alligators.

It is when the alligators are snapping, the current is running against you, and events are moving toward disaster that the true mettle of the power communicator is tested. Consider the following crises:

- You are the CEO of a large oil company, and one of your ships has just hit a shoal, releasing thousands of barrels of oil into environmentally sensitive waters.

- You are the top executive of an automobile company, and somebody discovers that some of the cars you have been selling as new are actually "executive cars" that have been driven thousands of miles but have had their odometers turned back to zero.

- You are in charge of a pharmaceutical company, and the public has just learned that someone with a twisted mind has slipped arsenic into the pain-killing capsules you market.

- You are the president of a major food chain that has sold improperly processed beef to its customers. A major outbreak of a severe illness, which has killed numerous people and produced the dangerous E. coli strain in countless others, has affected your customers in several western states.

The telephone rings. It is Stella Telstar from *Eyewitness News*. What do you do? You will need to follow three cardinal rules:

- **Accept responsibility.**

- **Tell the truth.**

- **Take immediate action.**

When you are less than honest with the media, you are being less than honest with the public you seek to serve. Your lack of candor will come back to haunt you. When a disaster strikes, do not try to pretend things are normal. Admit that a disaster has struck, do your best to put it into perspective, and tell what you are doing to deal with it.

The natural reaction, when you are in the middle of a crisis that could cast a negative light on you and your organization, is to keep a lid on it. However, what you should do is take the lead to inform the public, through the media, about the situation. If you avoid this assertive action, when they do reach you, print reporters will not just pocket their pencils and notebooks when you say "no comment." Electronic reporters will not pack away their mikes and cameras and head for the home studio.

Your "no comment" will send them on fact-finding expeditions that may yield (1) more negative publicity than you bargained for, or (2) wildly distorted information that makes the situation look far worse than it really is.

Prepare in Advance

To deal effectively with the public relations aspects of a disaster, you have to prepare in advance. Disasters, by their very nature, are unpredictable. If you are in charge of a chemical plant, you know that the potential exists for environmental spills, accidental atmospheric emissions, and harmful effects from toxic-waste dumps. So make sure that you or someone within your purview knows enough about these operations to talk intelligently with the media. Prepare a contingency plan that designates and prepares someone in authority either to answer the media's questions or to direct the media to someone who can answer them. Most major companies today have written policies that explain what to do and how to inform the public about emergencies.

Your crucial task is to deliver accurate information

to the media. Do this as soon as possible after the disaster has occurred. When possible, prepare media packets in advance. Let's use the chemical plant once more as an example. Your media packet could include background papers on what your plant produces, what constituents go into the products, and what chemical effects these products can have in specific concentrations. You will also want to explain the essential contributions these products make to an advanced society.

In addition to a media packet, you should have a designated spokesperson available to the media twenty-four hours a day. This person will need to have a clear understanding of the overall crisis and should have quick access to people with a technical understanding of the processes involved.

In disaster circumstances, do not fix the blame or divert it away from your organization. Rather, acknowledge the situation and demonstrate the company's concern over what is happening. Also, stress all company efforts to resolve the crisis expeditiously. Failure to give the media an accurate and quick account of what happened can result in a public relations disaster. This fiasco can compound the actual disaster.

The PR Tragedy of Three Mile Island

The owners of the Three Mile Island nuclear plant in Pennsylvania would probably tell you that the public relations disaster proved to be worse than the actual disaster that occurred there in 1979.

Douglas Bedell, an editorial writer for *The Bulletin* in Philadelphia during the Three Mile Island crisis, later became manager of media relations at Three Mile Island. In addition, he became manager of public information for General Public Utilities Corporation (GPU), the owner of Three Mile Island.

The near-disaster at the nuclear plant caught the utility company off guard and found it poorly prepared to handle the crisis situation. In 1987, Bedell wrote the following analysis of the disaster:

> GPU has acknowledged, time and again, that while radiation releases from the plant were minimal, it did not initially recognize the severity of the damage to the reactor system, and that it was unprepared to deal with the communications aspect of the accident. Within a few days, GPU *did* recognize that there was much to be learned from the Unit 2 accident. In a setting of crisis and collapsed credibility, it began assembling and applying those lessons.[1]

GPU paid a fearsome price for this early lack of preparedness. Editorial writers who dealt with the episode continued their attitude of distrust, as Bedell explained:

> Rather than sort through what went wrong, what worked and what didn't, what the problems were and what they weren't, the editorial writers remained in an unforgiving stance of distrust and dudgeon toward GPU. Not merely during the imme-

diate aftermath of the accident, but
throughout the excruciating, nearly six-
year period that preceded the successful
restart, in October 1985, of a modified
TMI Unit 1 under a significantly revamped
management system.[2]

It serves no purpose to blame the media for ignoring GPU's accomplishments after the disaster. You
have no control over the whims and foibles of the
media. But you *do* have control over your own operation and the way you handle your internal and exter-
nal communications about it.

Virginia Power Comes through . . . and Doesn't

Virginia Power Company had a less disastrous experience with public relations in its nuclear operations.
However, it once found itself in a situation that
required the company to mobilize its top executives to
put out some fires that should never have been lit.

The company had acquitted itself with honor during the early 1970s, when a welding supervisor for the
prime contractor on its Surry Nuclear Power Station
reported poor quality control in the welding of the
two-inch-thick stainless steel pipes in the reactor-core
cooling system. If the pipes suffered a total break and
the fuel rods lost all their cooling water, the emer-
gency cooling system would have only seconds in
which to replace the water. Otherwise, the reactor

would begin to melt down, with incalculable consequences.

When news of the quality-control glitches became public, the power company's public relations department made itself available to anyone from the media who sought information. If the public relations people could not answer questions, they gave the media names and telephone numbers of people who could answer them. The company eventually was required to make an audit of questionable welds, to replace some of them, and to submit to a stepped-up schedule of inspections once the plant went into operation.

Because the company cooperated fully with the media, the plant's side of the story was told: the chances of a total failure were very remote, even though the consequences of failure might have been dreadful; and the company was responsibly locating and correcting faulty welds.

Ironically, Virginia Power Company dropped the ball on a real disaster that it should have easily explained. Not long after the plant started generating electricity, three men working on some steam pipes in the power-generating plant were scalded when the pipes broke. They died as a result of the accident, which in no way was connected with the nuclear reactor. The pipes were not part of the core-cooling system; they were pipes that conveyed nonradioactive steam to the generating turbines. This was an unfortunate accident that could have happened as easily at a plant that burned coal, oil, or gas.

Smart public relations required that the company immediately inform the media of what had happened and how it had happened. Good PR would have emphasized, at the outset, that the accident had no connection whatever with the nuclear function. Instead, the company kept quiet until someone representing himself as knowledgeable about nuclear plants called a metropolitan newspaper with the "news" that the Surry plant had almost had a runaway reactor.

The company eventually had to call a news conference on the site of the disaster. A top corporate executive explained in detail what had happened and why the broken steam pipe posed no threat to anyone outside the immediate building. Unfortunately, when you are caught in a defensive response mode, often the best outcome you can expect is a neutral one.

Companies That Acted Effectively

We have seen a number of incidents of nationwide notoriety in which corporate executives took quick and effective action to defuse disaster situations.

Johnson & Johnson, the pharmaceutical giant, was the innocent victim of a vicious crime in which someone slipped poison into its Tylenol capsules. The company promptly took its product off the market, provided refunds for those who had already purchased it, and took steps to prevent future tampering with the product. Tylenol remained a viable product.

Lee Iacocca responded forthrightly when he learned that some Chrysler "executive" cars had their odometers run back to zero, then were sold as new cars. Iacocca issued a forceful statement in which he conceded that the practice was unethical, that Chrysler's top management did not approve of it, and that it would be discontinued immediately.

The Watergate Debacle

The premier example of how not to manage a crisis is the Watergate scandal of the 1970s.

The news was not the kind a president likes to hear during a reelection campaign. Some men had been caught in the act of burglarizing the offices of the Democratic National Committee in the Watergate complex. There were indications that the burglars had White House connections. Richard Nixon had two options:

1. He could have announced that his own investigation showed that the burglars were carrying out a mission authorized by people close to him. He could have expressed his shock and outrage at the incident and promised appropriate discipline for those who had gone so far. He could then have apologized to the American people.

2. He could have "stonewalled" it, trying to cover up the White House connection, and thus preventing Watergate from becoming a major issue in the 1972 presidential campaign.

Given Nixon's towering lead in the election polls at that time, the first strategy might have worked. The president probably would have won the election and, after a thorough shake-up in his administration, probably would have survived his second term.

We now know that the president chose to stonewall. The nation was treated to the pathetic spectacle of press secretary Ron Ziegler, manning the barricades against the relentless barrage of facts. He would issue a statement one day; and the next day, when it was contradicted by new information, he would declare that same statement "inoperative."

Do not get caught in such a situation. Give the public the truth as soon as you can verify it. Point out all the facts that reflect positively on your organization. Demonstrate your concern over what is happening and explain what you are doing about it. In this way, you retain a measure of influence over the information being disseminated. Once you choose to obstruct the media, you actually surrender any influence you might have over news coverage. The reporters who find you unresponsive will go looking for someone who *is* responsive. That someone may be on the opposite side of the issue from you. The other side has the opportunity to share its message, and when it comes time for your side to be told, the reporter will write, "A spokesman for Acme Amalgamated said the company would have no comment on the situation."

Heading Off Disasters

Sometimes you will be bringing your power communications to bear in heading off a disaster in the making.

When I was press secretary to Senator Harry Reid of Nevada, the senator recognized a crisis of confidence in this country. It involved the ongoing conflict between our citizens and the Internal Revenue Service. Reid heard horror story after horror story about how the IRS abused taxpayers. He decided to introduce "The Taxpayers' Bill of Rights" to offer protections to Americans. The bill he introduced sought a legislative remedy to years of abusive, and possibly illegal, actions by IRS agents. His bill was intended to put the taxpayer on equal footing with the IRS and, in this way, help avert the conflict from becoming a full-blown disaster. In a prepared statement, directly preceding a Senate hearing on the legislation, Reid said the following:

> The Taxpayers' Bill of Rights has one objective—to provide a legislative remedy for those people who have been abused or mistreated by overzealous Internal Revenue Service agents. This is a balanced piece of legislation. It preserves the ability of the IRS to collect taxes legally owed and also protects the individual taxpayers. It is *not anti*-IRS; it is *pro*-taxpayer.
>
> None of us are disputing our responsibility to pay taxes. However, this legislation is necessary because some IRS agents have forgotten the old saying, "The power to tax is *not* the power to destroy." It is my hope that the IRS will be reminded of the truth and wisdom contained in this statement. Equally important, I know that we have begun a legislative process—one that will prevent many of the degradations and financial tragedies previously suffered by the people of this nation.

The Taxpayers' Bill of Rights was signed into law by President Ronald Reagan on November 10, 1988. However, the senator did not wait for the legislation to be passed before aiming his power-communications cannons at it. He rolled out the guns as soon as he, along with two other senators, introduced the legislation.

Notice how Reid's statement was sprinkled with memorable phrases designed to inspire Americans: "to provide a legislative remedy for those people who have been abused or mistreated by overzealous Internal Revenue Service agents. . . . It is *not anti*-IRS; it is *pro*-taxpayer. . . . [and] will prevent many of the degradations and financial tragedies previously suffered by the people of this nation."

Reid responded to the critical issue while effectively addressing the three primary components of a forceful news release or statement. The content of the statement was *timely* because he made it in conjunction with a congressional hearing on the subject, which was scheduled within days of the annual federal tax deadline for most Americans. He satisfied the requirement of *distinctiveness* because the legislation was the first of its kind to offer such protections. The senator also fulfilled the third requisite of *impact* by discussing legislation that directly or indirectly would affect every person in the country.

Reid could send this statement anywhere in the United States with the realistic expectation that it would be used. Why? Because he was a public person whose leadership on this issue would positively affect people across the nation.

Handling Cynicism and Innuendo

The media and the public sometimes view issues cynically. With proper preparation, however, you can take much of the sting out of a negative development and turn it into a positive. You have the best chance to accomplish this with honesty and forthrightness.

When you are at the center of an event that threatens to damage your reputation or credibility, do not panic. Get the objective facts out as quickly as possible. Tell your side of the story. Let people know that you are concerned and are exerting your best efforts to deal with the situation. In the end, your candor and honesty will be rewarded.

At times, the best response you can give is no response. That is, let someone else speak on your behalf. Several years after I established my high-visibility consulting firm, I was contacted late one night by an advertising executive. He wanted me to help a local doctor who had recently lost a patient during surgery involving a breakthrough procedure. Because few people—especially the media—knew the details of the innovative technique, the reporters jumped all over the doctor, permeating their coverage with innuendo.

I worked with the doctor at several levels. I educated him about media skills, prepared his responses, and fielded all of his media calls.

In this scenario, I decided the doctor himself should not speak to the media. Because anything he might say under these stressful circumstances would become "public record," I did not want any extended remarks he might give to taint his defense in legal actions that would probably follow. My responses on his behalf included no information that could damage him; nor did I reveal specifics until such information was made public by official sources.

You might, at some time, find yourself in an equally critical situation that could be misconstrued by the inclusion of your remarks. Often, when confronted with a crisis, people react emotionally and want to respond immediately. It is important that, before responding, you look beyond the emotion-of-the-moment and understand the long-term effects of what you might say.

In Summary:

• Remember this cardinal rule when facing a crisis situation: Tell the truth.

• Once the media learn about a crisis situation, do not try to hide the facts. This avoidance can be fruitless and counterproductive.

• Get accurate information to the media as soon as possible after the disaster has occurred. If possible, make available media packets that provide valuable background information and details.

• Have a designated spokesperson available to the media twenty-four hours a day. This person must have a clear understanding of the overall crisis. The spokesperson also needs quick access to people with a technical understanding of the processes involved.

• When you are working to head off a negative situation, use news releases, news conferences, and other communications tools to get your message to the proper people in a forceful, forthright manner.

- At times, your best response is no response. That is, let someone else speak on your behalf.

Notes

1. Douglas Bedell, "TMI: Editorials Went Awry," *The Masthead: Quarterly Journal of the National Conference of Editorial Writers,* Spring 1987, 15.
2. Ibid.

11

Generating Your Own Public Personhood

Your name is the most important asset you possess. By "name" I am not referring merely to your given name at birth, or your family name, or your married name. I am referring to all the things that are associated with your name when people hear it or read it.

Your name is your reputation. This applies to businesses and organizations, as well as to individuals. When people hear or read your name, they should immediately make a positive association.

When people think of Abraham Lincoln, they immediately associate his name with honesty, compassion, the preservation of the Union, and the freeing of the slaves. With Albert Einstein, people think of a powerful intellect, the theories of relativity, and perhaps the formula $e = mc^2$. When people read the names of

Albert Schweitzer and Mother Teresa, they think of humanitarian service.

The name Rolls Royce creates images of expensive luxury automobiles. Porsche evokes thoughts of speed and superb handling. The word Xerox is synonymous with copying machines. Hewlett-Packard triggers the thought of top-notch computers.

What do people think of when they hear or read your name or the name of your organization?

Your task as a public person is to make sure that your name makes a positive impression on the people who live and work in your community. You want them to know you for the right reasons.

Decide What You Want to Be

First, you will need to decide what you want to do with your life and how you want people to think of you.

Floyd Wickman, one of the nation's leading sales trainers, spent about ten years as an enlisted man in the navy and a fruitless year in real estate before he decided on a career path. At a sales-training course he attended, he realized that real estate sales might provide him with career opportunities.

After completing the course, Wickman went back to his office and took out a business card his company kept on hand for new agents. Each card bore the name, address, and telephone number of the business. Below that was a blank place in which to type the new agent's name.

Floyd typed in the blank space, *Floyd Wickman, Million Dollar Club Member.* He attached it to the front of his desk so that everyone could see it. Having defined his image of himself, Floyd began doing the things that would fulfill the image. He sold more than a million dollars worth of real estate that year. He never had to pinch pennies again.[1]

Years later, after he had reached the top in real estate sales, Wickman was sitting in an audience of 2,300 people when he heard the speaker say, "One of you has greatness in you."

Wickman decided on the spot to become a successful speaker. That night, he wrote down on a piece of paper, "I will speak in front of 2,300 people by April 16, 1979." Wickman had given himself five years to reach his goal. He surpassed this goal within two months when he addressed 2,600 people.[2]

Wickman enjoyed his own success because he created a vision of exactly who he wanted to be and what he planned to accomplish. He had learned that waiting for his public personhood to evolve would cheat him of his full potential for personal and professional development. He knew that to excel, he had to create a forceful, positive vision. And he had to assert himself to make sure that the right people knew about it.

Each of us has to make a positive decision as to whom we want to become, in our individual and our organizational roles. We must create personal and organizational visions and commit ourselves to living them.

If your vision calls for becoming an exceptional salesperson, you must act as if the vision were already a reality. If your vision involves becoming a public person, you must act as if you already were a public person.

To get the most out of public personhood, you will benefit from positioning. To position yourself, you should first identify a community need that you can satisfy; then convince people that you are the best person to meet that need.

Establishing Credibility

You then look for methods of establishing your credibility with the public. To accomplish this, the community you want to influence should perceive you as knowledgeable about the need you are seeking to fill. You must inspire confidence in your ability to achieve it and convince people that you will act in their best interests.

If you want to achieve effective positioning, establish yourself as an expert. Then spread the word about your expertise through an information-dissemination program. You can choose to do this through a mass audience, a targeted audience, or both.

I worked with an attorney who had a thriving personal-injury practice. He wanted to do more in and for his community. He wanted professional visibility; he also wanted to provide helpful information to people who could benefit from his expertise.

We developed an entire high-visibility campaign with a three-pronged central theme: first, we assured people that they do not have to "succumb" to the legal process when they are already experiencing the pain of injury or loss. Second, we stressed that information and assistance are available. Third, we emphasized that this attorney—an expert—works in partnership with his clients to assure that their needs and expectations get top-notch attention.

We created a media plan that included news and feature releases. We produced a weekly public service program for television, which he anchored. We developed free seminars for him to teach at local colleges. We drafted speeches for him to present to civic organizations and professional associations. We also published collateral support materials for free distribution at these various high-visibility programs. All of these efforts provided a dynamic resource for the community and enhanced my client's visibility as "the expert" in his field.

Communicating about Pain

Another client—one of the country's most highly regarded pain-management physicians—contacted me for help. He was concerned about the proliferation of misinformation about pain treatment. He was very concerned that people would not seek viable help because of their fears and embarrassment about their pain.

We began our plan to position him as a media expert—that is, a media source—for stories that deal in any way with the subject of pain. Believe me, the media are packed with potential for these stories.

Initially, our efforts involved a substantial education campaign. We talked with editors and reporters about the impact of pain in our daily lives, the workplace, and elsewhere. It took awhile to convince the media that pain is one of the most universal experiences we encounter. Yet a chronic bout with pain will affect 80 percent of the people at some time in their lives.

We expanded on this fact to entice the media to incorporate my client in their story development. By reinforcing the universality of the problem and emphasizing his expertise and his credentials to speak about it, we established him as a visible medical expert in the media. Since then stories in which he appears as an expert source have appeared regularly on NBC television affiliates across the nation.

A word of caution: use judgment and legitimacy when establishing yourself as an expert source. Remember that your credibility is riding on this claim. If you do not have a broad enough knowledge of a subject and are called on to respond on that subject, you will never recover from an inaccurate, fuzzy, or shallow response. Know when *not* to respond.

Another thing to remember: do not try to establish yourself as an expert in too many areas. I once developed a high-profile campaign for one of my clients who owns a lucrative consulting business. For years, she had built her expertise in her field. She wanted a program that would position her as the consultant of choice in the minds of potential clients.

She gave me nearly a dozen complex "areas of expertise" that she wanted to promote. Each of these clustered specialties would stand alone. I counseled her to focus on no more than two or three specialties and do them well—as an expert. Very few people can perform a dozen tasks well, let alone as an expert. In this age of specialization, people no longer look for the jack of all trades. They look for the person who has specialized skills and has specific expertise.

Identify the areas that you know well. Identify also those areas that you do not know. Let go of what you do not know, or put it on a back shelf to supplement your specialty. My client did reduce her "exposure" and more than doubled her business in less than two years.

Getting the Word Out

Once you have developed your expertise, you will probably want to get the word out. This calls for targeting your message to the right audience or audiences.

One of my clients, Carson Construction Company, has built more than 3,000 commercial and industrial projects during its forty-eight–year history. When owner Doug Carson first contacted me, he was committed to developing a high-visibility program with two ongoing purposes. He wanted to educate the community about contributions made by the construction industry and his company and to eradicate long-held stereotypes about construction people.

We developed a multilevel program that included news and feature releases, guest columns, special community projects, involvement with nonprofit fund-raisers, and contributions to community programs.

One example of a special project, Play City, involved Carson in several ways. He cochaired the project, which comprised the efforts of several contractors and other construction industry associates. Carson, as past president of Big Brothers/Big Sisters, encouraged contractors to get involved in this nonprofit fund-raiser. The participants built playhouses that were auctioned off, and they raised more than $25,000 for the youth organization. Not only did Carson cochair the event, he also entered a playhouse, winning "Best of Show" honors. We distributed news releases about the event that appeared several times in the media.

This project demonstrates how you can make a contribution to your community and, at the same time, create positive visibility for yourself or your company. We were able to generate media coverage like this about once a month by targeting our messages to newspapers, television, and trade publications. We always kept in mind the purpose of our communication and which people we wanted to receive that message. This special media focus helped us profile my client and his company as people who care about the community and want to make a difference in its progress.

Getting Other People to Work for You

One of the most effective kinds of public exposure is endorsements from other people. Some of the most beneficial endorsements originate with credible, friendly competitors. The world of athletics provides many examples of this. While I was working with the

Runnin' Rebels, the 1990 NCAA basketball champions from the University of Nevada-Las Vegas, competing coaches often praised the Rebels and their coaching staff. Numerous coaches would credit our team with a victory, or even praise us after our own loss.

You want unsolicited positive endorsements wherever possible from friendly competitors or die-hard supporters. Your skills, talents, and expertise can receive no higher praise than that produced through testimonials. When the *un*solicited remark is not available, however, do not hesitate to seek out endorsers to say a nice word or two about you in some public forum. This provides the dispersal of positive points about you—points that you cannot comfortably make about yourself.

In creating a positive personhood for yourself, you also do not want to forget the value of a spouse or other family member with an individual identity.

In both 1986 and 1988, I helped develop and administer spousal programs for Landra Reid and Bonnie Bryan, wives of Harry Reid and Richard Bryan, candidates for the United States Senate. These programs were among the first of their type in the nation.

As the two candidates developed their own campaign strategies, I worked on complementary but individual platforms for their wives. This gave the candidates double strength, and twice as much exposure in trying to reach the voters. Each of the wives established her own identity, issues, and media skills. Each built her own constituencies to supplement and complement those that her husband was building. Of equal importance, I helped each wife recognize that her contributions were as essential to the campaign as those of her husband.

The spousal programs worked. Both Senate candidates were elected to represent Nevada in Washington. Each newly elected senator gave full credit to his wife for the invaluable contributions her campaign involvement made to the election victory. It is clear that because each candidate was already holding office—Reid was a congressman and Bryan was governor—that spousal involvement was crucial. While the candidates performed their daily elective duties, their spouses were able to meet with voters across the state. These elections were successful because of the combined efforts of the candidates and their spouses.

In the corporate world, this same principle applies as more and more spouses—men and women—take on responsible public roles and must be intelligent about their own public appearances and positioning. This duality gives clients or constituents the opportunity to experience more depth in their relationships with these leaders. It also gives the media a broader focus.

Promoting Yourself as a Public Speaker

Public speaking, as I mentioned in chapter 9, is an important communication tool for public persons. In addition to needing presentation skills to deliver your message effectively to certain audiences, you can use your speaking abilities to create high-profile exposure for you and your expertise in the community.

If your company or organization has a speakers

bureau, volunteer yourself as a speaker. If you have expertise in a subject of public interest, contact the program chairperson of the civic clubs in your community, or the community college or university continuing education program. Let them know that you are available. They are always looking for interesting presenters.

Management consultant Jeffrey P. Davidson started his speaking career by looking through the local paper for notices of professional meetings. Davidson said:

> I called the meeting planners listed and suggested that their members might benefit from my presentation. Often, I did this for no fee. My compensation was developing my speaking skills, gaining exposure within the professional community, and converting tape transcripts into articles for publications.[3]

Remember that when a group invites you to speak, it is not offering you a chance to get in a free commercial or make a direct sales pitch. You are there to share your knowledge and expertise and to leave your audience with good feelings about you and your organization. As Davidson observes:

> Your decision on whether to seek speaking engagements as a personal promotional tool hinges on your ability to be interesting and to have something worthwhile to say to a group composed of targets of opportunity or influence.[4]

You may realize no immediate tangible gains from a public speech. Few speeches yield that kind of instant payoff. But the impression you make can be a lasting one. Do not be surprised if, years later, a prospective client comes to you and says, "I remember you from that speech you gave back in 1994."

When you make a commitment to speak to an organization, you also have the opportunity to promote your presentation to the membership, and even the entire community, prior to your speaking event. Most organizations will make some effort to let their members know when and where you are going to speak. But do not rely solely on your hosts to promote you. Host organizations, many of which rely on volunteer support, often neglect to publicize your program. Therefore, do not hesitate to take the initiative in promoting your speech.

You can ask your hosts whether you can submit an article for the organization's newsletter. Find out whether it is all right for you to issue advance news releases and invite the media to attend. If the organization does not object, send out news releases to the local media about three weeks in advance of the event. For the trade media, check the editorial deadlines and time your releases accordingly. If the organization does not object, enclose a letter with each release inviting the editor to attend. You might also consider sending out advance texts, or at least significant excerpts, of your speech.

Most organizations send out meeting notices, but these often bear close resemblances to junk mail and are overlooked and discarded. Ask your host to send you copies of the last few meeting announcements. If they look too run-of-the-mill, offer to prepare your own announcement. Put some imagination into the design and include the same information you would put into a news release. Show how your presentation will be different, appealing, and useful.

Learning Self-Promotion from Politics

When you are in politics, self-promotion is not just an important sideline; it is your key to staying in office. That is why members of Congress, governors, and other important public figures have press secretaries and other aides to help keep them before the public in positive ways.

Not every public person needs the elaborate system for self-promotion that a state or national political figure needs. Fortunately, the techniques such high-visibility leaders utilize can help those who want to undertake their own self-promotional programs.

As press secretary to Senator Harry Reid of Nevada, I set up a system for following up on every opportunity to bring the senator's name before the public. We used news releases and news statements, written in broadcast-writing style. We took advantage of short speeches on the Senate floor, alerting state television stations so that they could record them for later play in newscasts. We often reprinted statements made in these speeches for later constituent mailings to reinforce the senator's position on issues.

We used radio and television interviews and satellite feeds. Often, stations across the country contract with Washington, D.C., television companies to do interviews in the office or on location. It is the job of the press secretary to get the outline of the interview in advance and brief the senator, preparing him in terms of content and direction. The press secretary also makes sure that the member is properly dressed, has his make-up on, and postures himself correctly.

The press secretary also keeps alert about special-interest publications toward which the senator can target his message. The options for impact are as diverse as the interests represented by the publications. If the publication is targeted toward blacks, Hispanics, university students, mobile-home owners, or retirees, the press secretary can tailor a column or article to address the group's specific interests and problems.

Public persons of all types can take a cue here. Think of the different groups that can benefit from your expertise: do these groups have publications prepared specifically for them? Prepare articles in your field of expertise that demonstrate your knowledge of their problems and your ability to help them.

You can also develop your own newsletter to promote you or your organization. Congressional members send newsletters regularly to their constituents. They use these tools to inform the voters about activities in key areas and how they, as public officials, are representing the public's best interests. For a public person in private business, the newsletter can be an effective medium for keeping your name before potential customers and clients.

Frequently, governmental bodies, organizations, and other groups would ask the senator to record a testimony, speech, tribute, public service announcement, or other videotaped product for their use at events or for public service television purposes.

Through the videotape, his image was able to go places in the state where he could not be physically present.

Audio presentations offered powerful returns for the small amount of time we invested in them. Sometimes, the senator would record a public service announcement. At other times, he would use the audiotape like a videotape to carry a particular message to a meeting or other public gathering.

The public person whose power base is rooted in the private business world can also make use of video presentations. In fact, media skills have become essential for successful managers and executives during the nineties. Video presentations allow you to introduce new product lines to nationwide sales forces. Video cassettes and video laser discs allow for a professional, uniform presentation conveying the same information to everyone everywhere. Sales training can also be conducted via video cassette or disc. Executives even package their resumes in the form of video presentations.

Staying Well Informed

A United States senator always has to appear well informed. It is the press secretary's responsibility to keep the senator briefed on all the issues likely to surface when he or she faces the media and constituent groups.

This need requires that the press secretary be a daily collector of news. As Senator Reid's press secretary, I received news daily by fax from his offices around Nevada. Each office would send me important information from its area to keep the senator and his staff informed.

I also had newspapers from around the state mailed to the Washington office so that I could review them, track important issues, and keep a clip file for the senator. In addition, I monitored the Washington press and other national media. I gave the senator a news briefing and news clips from important editorials and news articles before 9 A.M. daily.

As a public person in your own community, you may not be faced with the necessity of dealing with a statewide constituency from an outpost in Washington. However, it is important that you keep up with developments that affect the people you serve.

Media can be a rich source of information. You may not need to monitor high-profile media for minute-by-minute coverage of issues. However, as a businessperson, you may want to read the *Wall Street Journal, Forbes,* and other financial publications. And national news magazines, such as *Time, Newsweek,* and *U.S. News & World Report,* can help keep you well informed about national and international issues. Do not underestimate, too, the powerful information you can assimilate from twenty-four-hour news channels on radio and television. As you read, listen, and watch, ask yourself, "What in this story is important for me to know?"

In addition to national and international affairs, you will need to know important facts about the community or communities in which you function as a public person. To be well rounded, you should read your local newspaper and at least one newspaper that does a comprehensive job of covering your state. The people with whom you deal must perceive you as a knowledgeable person who not only knows their problems but also cares about people and how their needs can be met.

Correspondence That Shows You Care

The senator liked to reach out to people through letters of congratulations. Therefore, I urged his staffers all around Nevada to read newspapers carefully for articles involving people and groups in the community. We looked for articles about the police lieutenant who was promoted to captain, the teacher who received a twenty-year pin, the mother who was elected president of the local PTA, the student who was named speller of the year, the young man who made Eagle Scout, or the athlete named most valuable player. The senator would send these "stars" congratulatory letters.

Look for such stories in your local newspaper. Take the time to write personal letters of congratulation. You might have a form letter prepared and stored on your computer that you could easily modify and personalize to fit each recipient.

Demonstrating your leadership is also important in times of grief. Read the obituary columns. You need not confine expressions of sympathy to personal friends. Whenever a widely known local person dies, it presents you with an opportunity to express your caring and concern. It could be a young person who dies in an accident, a long-time educator, a respected minister, or some other person who has affected you or your community directly or indirectly.

Births and anniversaries offer happier occasions for sending greetings. A card or note on such occasions can enhance your positioning with the recipients and create a reservoir of good will toward you. Senator Reid was fond of sending out such greetings. Be particularly alert for fiftieth wedding anniversaries and ninetieth or one-hundredth birthdays. Greetings sent on such occasions are likely to be shared with entire families—and extended families can be quite large.

Just a Reminder

If you look for them you will find a wealth of opportunities to put your name before the public in a favorable light. The formula for becoming a positive public person is simple enough: find something good to do and do it well. Then let the public know what you are doing. You will be rewarded with a satisfying sense of accomplishment and the gratification that comes from public recognition of your good deeds. And the community will benefit as the recipient of your contributions.

In Summary:

- To promote your public personhood, make sure that your name is known in the community in which you move, and make sure that it is known for the right reasons.

- To begin building a good name, first decide what you want to do with your life and how you want to do it. Create a personal and organizational vision, make a commitment to it, and live it.

- To spotlight yourself as a public person requires effective positioning. To promote yourself, identify a need that you can satisfy, then set out to demonstrate to people how you can resolve it.

- Look for methods to establish your credibility with the public. To accomplish this, your community must perceive you as knowledgeable about what you plan to achieve and inspire confidence in your ability to do so. You will also need to convince people that you will act in their best interests.

- One effective approach to self-promotion focuses on establishing yourself as an expert. You then put your expertise to work gaining recognition for yourself through mass audiences.

- Do not claim to be an expert unless you have the requisite expertise. Also, avoid the tendency to try to establish yourself as an expert in too many areas.

- Getting the word out about yourself calls for skills in reaching mass audiences and targeted audiences through media releases and other devices.

- A spouse or other family member with an individual identity can be a valuable asset in creating a favorable public identity for you and your organization.

- Speaking to civic and professional audiences provides you with opportunities for positive profiling in your self-promotional efforts.

- Individuals seeking to build public personhood can learn from the structured way a successful politician goes about it.

- Nevada Senator Harry Reid made use of news releases, newsletters, radio and television feeds, videotapes, audiotapes, and public-speaking opportunities.

- Daily newspapers, as well as radio and television, offer rich sources of opportunities for self-promotion.

- You can use the media to:

  1. Identify people to whom you might appropriately send congratulatory notes or letters of sympathy and condolence.
  2. Inform yourself about issues that will help you connect with the people you are trying to reach.

Notes

1. Floyd Wickman, *The Wickman Formula: Seven Steps to Achieving Your Full Potential* (Detroit: Floyd Wickman Associates, 1991), 96, 119–20.
2. Ibid., 121.
3. Jeffrey P. Davidson, *Blow Your Own Horn: How to Market Yourself and Your Career* (New York: Amacom, 1987), 160.
4. Ibid.

Epilogue

The story is told about the taciturn New England farmer who, in a rash moment arising from a rare indulgence in strong drink, once confided to a friend: "You know, Ginny is about the best wife a man could ever have. Sometimes I love her so much it's all I can do to keep from telling her."

Think of the rich pleasures the husband and his wife have missed because he resisted that impulse to communicate! You too can be missing out on opportunities to reach out to others if you have failed to cultivate your powers of communication.

Let's consider how this principle might apply to business. A billion-dollar project will be assigned to either Corporation X or Corporation Y. The assignment of the contract depends on the most timely and cost-effective resolution of certain hypotheticals.

One hundred middle and top managers from Corporation X comprise a think tank, which is organized into teams of ten. Each team is assigned a specific task and is isolated from the other nine. Unfortunately, this isolation also precludes them from communicating with one other.

Corporation Y has created just one team of twenty to tackle the assignment. Individually, all 120 problem-solvers from both companies are intellectually matched. Therefore, when the work of Corporation Y, with its twenty participants, is compared to any one of Corporation X's ten-member teams, Corporation Y surpasses Corporation X in terms of intellect and time. Eventually, by taking on one team at a time, Corporation Y quickly prevails and eventually wins the contract.

The ability to communicate would have multiplied the power of that one-hundred-member team. A coordination of intelligence between the ten teams would have probably obliterated Corporation Y's team of twenty very quickly. By consolidating its efforts, the strength of numbers could have been applied and helped Corporation X at the critical point.

Communication breaks down the barriers to action and focuses the means to act. This is true whether you are dealing with a political force, a corporate entity, or a community organization. Effective communication multiplies your power. And, as John Milton observed, "Good, the more communicated, the more abundant grows."

This book has been intended to help you communicate constructively so that you can maximize your power and communicate the good that you do so that it "more abundant grows."

I hope that this book will help you, in powerful and positive ways, to reach out to others in your organization, your community, and the world. Equally important, I hope that you find or create many opportunities to spread the news about your accomplishments so that others will know of your deeds, respect them, and emulate them.

Bibliography

Aburdene, Patricia. "How to Think Like a CEO for the '90s." *Working Woman*, September 1990, 134–37.

Alexander, Roy. *Power Speech: The Quickest Route to Business and Personal Success.* New York: Amacom, 1986.

Anderson, James B. *Speaking to Groups Eyeball to Eyeball.* Vienna, Va.: Wyndmoor Press, 1989.

Aronoff, Craig E. *Business and the Media.* Santa Monica, Cal.: Goodyear Publishing, 1979.

Bartlett, John. *Familiar Quotations.* Edited by Emily Morrison Beck and the editorial staff of Little, Brown and Company, Boston: Little, Brown, and Company 1980.

Bates, Stephen. *If No News, Send Rumors.* New York: St. Martin's Press, 1989.

Bedell, Douglas. "TMI: Editorials Went Awry." *The Masthead: Quarterly Journal of the National Conference of Editorial Writers* (Spring 1987): 14–46.

Bramson, Robert M. *Coping with Difficult People.* New York: Doubleday, 1981.

Brody, E. W. *Communicating for Survival: Coping with Diminishing Human Resources.* Westport, Conn.: Greenwood Publishing Group, 1987.

———. *Professional Practice Development: From Planning to Crisis*

Response. Westport, Conn.: Greenwood Publishing Group, 1989.

———. *Communication Tomorrow: New Audiences, New Technologies, New Media.* Westport, Conn.: Greenwood Publishing Group, 1990.

———. *Managing Communication Processes: From Planning to Crisis Response.* Westport, Conn.: Greenwood Publishing Group, 1991.

Brown, Mary Helen, and Floyd, Kathy. *Activities in Professional Communication.* Dubuque, Ia.: Kendall/Hunt Publishing, 1990.

Burgett, Gordon. *Empire-Building.* Santa Maria, Cal.: Communication Unlimited, 1987.

Byrd, Donald and Cabetas, Isis C. *React Interact.* New York: Prentice Hall, 1991.

Caroselli, Marlene. *Communicate with Quality.* Culver City, Cal.: Center for Professional Development, 1990.

———. *The Language of Leadership.* Amherst, Mass.: Human Resource Development Press, 1990.

Chancellor, John, and Walter R. Mears. *The News Business.* New York: Harper and Row, 1983.

Cohen, Herb. *You Can Negotiate Anything.* Toronto: Bantam Books, 1980.

Davidson, Jeffrey P. *Blow Your Own Horn: How to Market Yourself and Your Career.* New York: Amacom, 1987.

Detz, Joan. *How to Write and Give a Speech.* New York: St. Martin's Press, 1984.

Fast, Julius. *Body Language: The Essential Secrets of Non-Verbal Communication.* New York: MJF Books, 1970.

Fast, Julius, and Barbara Fast. *Talking between the Lines: How We Mean More Than We Say.* New York: Viking Press, 1979.

Frank, Milo O. *How to Get Your Point Across in 30 Seconds or Less.* New York: Pocket Books, 1986.

Fritz, Roger. *You're in Charge: A Guide for Business and Personal Success.* Glenview, Ill.: Scott, Foresman, 1986.

Fry, Ron. *101 Great Answers to the Toughest Interview Questions.* Hawthorne, N.J.: Career Press, 1991.

Handley, Cathy. *10 Days to Miracle Speech Power.* New York: Parker Publishing, 1979.

Heldmann, Mary L. *When Words Hurt.* New York: New Chapter Press, 1988.

Hilton, Jack, and Mary Knoblauch. *On Television: A Survival Guide for Media Interviews.* New York: Amacom, 1980.

Klepper, Michael M. *Getting Your Message Out: How to Get Use, and Survive Radio and Television Air Time*. Englewood Cliffs, N.J.: Prentice Hall, 1984.

Kouzes, James M. and Barry Z. Posner, "The Credibility Factor: What Followers Expect from Their Leaders." *Management Review* (January 1990): 29–33.

Kushner, Malcolm. *The Light Touch: How to Use Humor for Business Success*. New York: Simon and Schuster, 1990.

Lenson, Barry. *Executive Leadership through Communication*. New York: National Institute of Business Management, 1990.

Machan, Dyan. "Do You Sincerely Want To Be Funny?" *Forbes*, October 15, 1990, 212–14.

Martel, Myles. *Mastering the Art of Q and A: A Survival Guide for Tough, Trick, and Hostile Questions*. Homewood, Ill.: Dow Jones-Irwin, 1989.

McCarthy, Michael J. *Mastering the Information Age*. Los Angeles: Jeremy P. Tarcher, 1990.

Molloy, John T. *How to Work the Competition into the Ground and Have Fun Doing It*. New York: Warner Books, 1987.

Nierenberg, Gerald I., and Henry H. Calero. *How to Read a Person Like a Book*. New York: Pocket Books, 1971.

Parkhurst, William. *The Eloquent Executive*. New York: Times Books, 1988.

Peale, Norman Vincent. *Positive Imaging: The Powerful Way to Change Your Life*. New York: Fawcett Crest, 1982.

Qubein, Nido R. *Communicate Like a Pro*. New York: Berkeley Books, 1983.

———. *Get the Best from Yourself: The Complete System of Personal and Professional Development*. Englewood Cliffs, N.J.: Prentice Hall, 1983.

———. *Professional Selling Techniques*. New York: Farnesworth Publishing, 1983.

Rafe, Stephen C. *How to Be Prepared to Think on Your Feet*. New York: Harper Business, 1990.

Rein, Irving, Philip Kotler, and Martin Stoller. *High Visibility*. New York: Dodd, Mead, 1987.

Robbins, H. *How to Speak and Listen Effectively*. New York: Amacom, 1992.

Shields, Donald J., Donald G. Shields, and Lela K. Bullerdick. *Effective Communications for Professionals*. Dubuque, Ia.: Kendall/Hunt Publishing, 1989.

Smith, Terry C. *Making Successful Presentations*. New York: John Wiley and Sons, 1984.

Vassallo, Wanda, and Dean Angel. *How to Handle the News Media.* Cincinnati: Betterway Books, 1992.

Walters, Dottie, and Lilly Walters. *Speak and Grow Rich.* Englewood Cliffs, N.J.: Prentice Hall, 1989.

Walton, Donald. *Are You Communicating?* New York: McGraw-Hill, 1989.

Wickman, Floyd. *The Wickman Formula: Seven Steps to Achieving Your Full Potential.* Detroit: Floyd Wickman Associates, 1991.

Woodall, Marian. *Thinking on Your Feet: Answering Questions Well Whether You Know the Answer or Not.* Lake Oswego, Ore.: Professional Business Communications, 1987.

Zorn, Dennis. H. *Communicating . . . Isn't Just Talking! The Art and Power of Communications for the Professional and the Individual.* San Leandro, Cal.: Trilogy Enterprize, 1990.

Index

Latin, 55, 69; loaded, 198; longer, 56; of mouth, 2, 111; multisyllabic, 55, 59; offending, 199; positive impact, 56; power-laden, 53; processors, 130; shorter, 55–56; spoken, 26; spreading, 254; unfamiliar, 68, 70; understandable, 59; use simple, 217, 232; vague, 61; weighing, 161; well-understood, 69

Work sheet, 210

Writing, 10, 63, 69, 91, 104–5, 119, 124, 126, 133–34, 144, 212; actual, 212; broadcast, 263, news release, 125, 134, 137; of news stories, 134; persuasive, 13; speech, 212, 217